Biodiversity

Other Books in the Current Controversies Series

Blogs

Capital Punishment

Developing Nations

Domestic Wiretapping

Drug Trafficking

Espionage and Intelligence

Food

Global Warming

Homosexuality

Illegal Immigration

Online Social Networking

Pollution

Prescription Drugs

Rap Music and Culture

School Violence

The Middle East

The Wage Gap

Urban Sprawl

Violence Against Women

Biodiversity

Debra A. Miller, Book Editor

GREENHAVEN PRESS
A part of Gale, Cengage Learning

Detroit • New York • San Francisco • New Haven, Conn • Waterville, Maine • London

Christine Nasso, *Publisher*
Elizabeth Des Chenes, *Managing Editor*

For more information, contact:
Greenhaven Press
27500 Drake Rd.
Farmington Hills, MI 48331-3535
Or you can visit our Internet site at gale.cengage.com

For product information and technology assistance, contact us at

Gale Customer Support, 1-800-877-4253
For permission to use material from this text or product, submit all requests online at www.cengage.com/permissions

Further permissions questions can be emailed to permissionrequest@cengage.com

Articles in Greenhaven Press anthologies are often edited for length to meet page requirements. In addition, original titles of these works are changed to clearly present the main thesis and to explicitly indicate the author's opinion. Every effort is made to ensure that Greenhaven Press accurately reflects the original intent of the authors. Every effort has been made to trace the owners of copyrighted material.

Cover image copyright Szefei, 2008. Used under license from Shutterstock.com.

LIBRARY OF CONGRESS CATALOGING-IN-PUBLICATION DATA

Biodiversity / Debra A. Miller, book editor.
   p. cm. -- (Current controversies)
  Includes bibliographical references and index.
  ISBN-13: 978-0-7377-3952-7 (hardcover)
  ISBN-10: 0-7377-3952-5 (hardcover)
  ISBN-13: 978-0-7377-3953-4 (pbk.)
  ISBN-10: 0-7377-3953-3 (pbk.)
  1. Biodiversity--Juvenile literature. I. Miller, Debra A.
  QH541.15.B56B557 2008
  333.95--dc22

                        2008002349

Printed in the United States of America
1 2 3 4 5   12 11 10 09 08

ED135

Contents

Foreword   **13**

Introduction   **16**

Chapter 1: Is Biodiversity Loss a Serious Problem?

Biodiversity: An Overview   **21**

Environmental Literacy Council

Biodiversity is important because it provides ecosystem support, food, and medicines, as well as a legacy of natural beauty for future generations.

Yes: Biodiversity Loss Is a Serious Problem

The Earth Is on the Verge of a   **24**
Global Biodiversity Catastrophe

Steve Connor

According to some of the world's most eminent scientists, the Earth is facing a global emergency in which all aspects of biodiversity are in serious decline, and a large number of populations and species are likely to become extinct this century.

Biodiversity Is Essential to Every Aspect   **28**
of Human Life

U.S. Agency for International Development

Biodiversity provides food, medicine, clean air, and clean water and is the foundation for all the Earth's essential goods and services—economic benefits worth at least $3 trillion per year.

Biodiversity Is Important to Medicine,   **31**
Bioengineering, and Health Care

Julie Majeres

Wild plants and animals are the source of biochemicals used to develop many life-saving drugs, and they also provide other scientific, economic, and recreational benefits.

Marine Biodiversity Just as Important   39
as Land Diversity
The Economist

Marine biodiversity matters because a wide variety of sea
life is necessary to maintain water quality, process nutrients, and keep the oceans healthy—both for humans and
for fish products harvested from the seas.

No: Biodiversity Loss Is Not a Serious Problem

Scientific Study of Biodiversity Decline   43
Is Still in the Early Stages
Shahid Naeem

Researchers agree that a healthy ecosystem requires a
high level of biodiversity, but how much biodiversity is
needed to ensure that ecosystems are healthy and life-
sustaining is still the subject of considerable debate and
study.

Dire Predictions of a Biodiversity Crisis   53
May Be Overstated
Rhett A. Butler

Although most scientists agree that biodiversity is declining, the degree to which it will occur in the future has
long been the subject of debate, and some of the most
dire predictions may be overstated.

Biodiversity May Rise and Decline as Part   63
of a Natural Earth Cycle
Space Daily

A study of the fossil records of marine animals over the
past 542 million years suggests that biodiversity rises and
falls in cycles of 62 million years.

Chapter 2: What Plant and Animal Species Are Going Extinct?

Chapter Preface   68

Without Action, Many Plant and Animal   71
Species Will Likely Be Extinct in Fifty Years
Philip Seaton

Unless urgent action is taken, activities such as logging of forests, conversion of forests to agriculture, illegal hunting, and global warming will decimate many of the Earth's plant and animal species.

All Wild Fisheries May Be Extinct by 2050   **75**
Environment News Service
Scientists warn that the loss of biodiversity is rapidly reducing the ocean's ability to produce seafood, resist diseases, filter pollutants, and rebound from stresses such as overfishing and climate change.

200-Year-Old Tropical Rainforests Are   **80**
Disappearing at a Rate Never Seen Before
Geographical
The world's tropical rainforests are the Earth's largest reservoir of biological diversity, containing more than half of its plant and animal species, but they have been vastly reduced in size in the last 200 years by agriculture.

Acid Oceans May Kill Off the World's   **85**
Coral Reefs
Juliet Eilperin
Rising levels of carbon dioxide in the atmosphere are making the world's oceans more acidic, and by the end of the century, this trend could decimate coral reefs and creatures that form the foundation for the ocean's food systems.

America's Wild Bird Populations   **90**
Are Declining
National Audubon Society
Populations of some of America's most familiar and beloved birds have dramatically declined over the past forty years, some as much as 80 percent, due to the loss of grasslands, forests, wetlands, and other critical habitats, and this sends a serious message about biodiversity loss.

The Risk of Species Extinction Is Increasing   **95**
Due to Global Warming
John Roach
A recent study predicts that, by 2050, rising temperatures caused by the human production of carbon dioxide and other greenhouse gases could destroy more than a million plant and animal species.

Chapter 3: Are Food Production Activities Harming the Earth's Biodiversity?

Chapter Preface   **100**

Yes: Food Production Activities Are Harming the Earth's Biodiversity

Industrial Agriculture Is One of the Main   **103**
Threats to Biodiversity

   Miguel A. Altieri

   Modern agriculture, especially monoculture—the practice of farming just one or two crops, changes the environment over vast areas, replacing nature's diversity with
   a tiny number of plants and animals.

Biotechnology Is a Threat to Biodiversity   **113**

   David Kennell

   Genetically engineered crops will greatly accelerate the
   decline of biodiversity in the plant world because they
   replace native crops with a monoculture system of agriculture that disrupts normal ecology with many unknown
   consequences.

Overfishing Is the Biggest Threat to   **118**
Marine Biodiversity

   United Nations Environment Programme

   Fishing provides a livelihood and food security for more
   than 200 million people, but the rapid growth in demand for fish products is depleting fish populations and
   destroying entire ecosystems.

No: Food Production Activities Are Not Harming the Earth's Biodiversity

High-Yield, Industrial Agriculture   **121**
Protects Biodiversity

   Center for Global Food Issues

   Growing more crops and trees per acre through high-
   yield agriculture leaves more land for nature and prevents further deforestation to create farmland for organic
   or more primitive methods of farming.

Biotechnology Is Not a Threat   124
to Biodiversity
Michael Howie

It is a myth that genetically engineered crops will lower
biodiversity; in fact, biotechnology may improve and
protect biodiversity by not only saving land but also by
using biodiversity to improve agriculture in the long-
term.

Commercial Fishing Is Not Significantly   128
Affecting the Oceans' Biodiversity
Jerry Fraser

Commercial fishing is just one of several factors that affect marine biodiversity, and it will likely produce the
fewest adverse impacts; other factors such as pollution,
habitat destruction, and climate change must also be addressed to protect the oceans.

Chapter 4: How Can the Earth's Biodiversity Be Preserved?

Chapter Preface   132

Conservation Efforts Should Target   135
Biodiversity "Hotspots"
Peter A. Seligmann

The world is facing a biodiversity crisis, but tackling a
problem of this scale and complexity, often with modest
funds, requires study and protection of targeted
"hotspots"—regions that have the richest varieties of
plant and animal species.

Green Development Offers a Way   138
to Save Biodiversity
Noel Castree

Green development—the concept of rich countries, corporations, or ecotourists paying developing nations not
to destroy natural resources—provides the revenue to
protect biodiversity, but so far problems have plagued
these projects in practice.

The Convention on Biological Diversity   **145**
Is Helping to Preserve Biodiversity
Secretariat of the Convention
on Biological Diversity

The Convention on Biological Diversity, an international
treaty signed by more than 170 countries, is helping to
shape global action on biodiversity by promoting the
philosophy of sustainable development.

The Rainforests Can Be Saved with   **155**
Sustainable Logging and Agriculture
The Economist

A new approach to saving the rainforests is being adopted
in Brazil—subsidies and tax incentives that favor deforestation are removed and forests are treated as a sustainable resource that can yield lumber and other forest products.

Following Natural Design Principles   **159**
Can Protect Biodiversity
William McDonough

By eliminating waste, through the production of goods
that are biodegradable or that are constantly recycled,
humans can live by the laws of nature and protect the
Earth's biodiversity.

Smarter Management of the Oceans   **164**
Would Allow Sea Life to Rebound
Ben Carmichael

By creating protected marine areas similar to wildlife
preserves on land, stopping overfishing, and making wise
management decisions about our use of the seas, humans
can protect the oceans' rich biodiversity.

Reducing the Human Population   **167**
While Expanding Conservation Practices
Provides the Best Chances for Reversing
Biodiversity Loss
Tatiana Siegel

Limiting the human population growth of approximately
73 million births per year, and adopting lifestyle behav-
iors that conserve resources may be the most viable strategies for avoiding a global biodiversity cataclysm.

Stabilizing the Human Population   174
by Empowering Women Can Help
Protect Biodiversity
    Mia MacDonald and Danielle Nierenberg
    Fertility rates are highest in developing countries that
    have the most biodiversity, but empowering women by
    providing education and improving their social status
    can help to limit population growth and protect biodi-
    versity resources.

Organizations to Contact   179

Bibliography   184

Index   190

Foreword

By definition, controversies are "discussions of questions in which opposing opinions clash" (Webster's Twentieth Century Dictionary Unabridged). Few would deny that controversies are a pervasive part of the human condition and exist on virtually every level of human enterprise. Controversies transpire between individuals and among groups, within nations and between nations. Controversies supply the grist necessary for progress by providing challenges and challengers to the status quo. They also create atmospheres where strife and warfare can flourish. A world without controversies would be a peaceful world; but it also would be, by and large, static and prosaic.

The Series' Purpose

The purpose of the Current Controversies series is to explore many of the social, political, and economic controversies dominating the national and international scenes today. Titles selected for inclusion in the series are highly focused and specific. For example, from the larger category of criminal justice, Current Controversies deals with specific topics such as police brutality, gun control, white collar crime, and others. The debates in Current Controversies also are presented in a useful, timeless fashion. Articles and book excerpts included in each title are selected if they contribute valuable, long-range ideas to the overall debate. And wherever possible, current information is enhanced with historical documents and other relevant materials. Thus, while individual titles are current in focus, every effort is made to ensure that they will not become quickly outdated. Books in the Current Controversies series will remain important resources for librarians, teachers, and students for many years.

In addition to keeping the titles focused and specific, great care is taken in the editorial format of each book in the series. Book introductions and chapter prefaces are offered to provide background material for readers. Chapters are organized around several key questions that are answered with diverse opinions representing all points on the political spectrum. Materials in each chapter include opinions in which authors clearly disagree as well as alternative opinions in which authors may agree on a broader issue but disagree on the possible solutions. In this way, the content of each volume in Current Controversies mirrors the mosaic of opinions encountered in society. Readers will quickly realize that there are many viable answers to these complex issues. By questioning each author's conclusions, students and casual readers can begin to develop the critical thinking skills so important to evaluating opinionated material.

Current Controversies is also ideal for controlled research. Each anthology in the series is composed of primary sources taken from a wide gamut of informational categories including periodicals, newspapers, books, U.S. and foreign government documents, and the publications of private and public organizations. Readers will find factual support for reports, debates, and research papers covering all areas of important issues. In addition, an annotated table of contents, an index, a book and periodical bibliography, and a list of organizations to contact are included in each book to expedite further research.

Perhaps more than ever before in history, people are confronted with diverse and contradictory information. During the Persian Gulf War, for example, the public was not only treated to minute-to-minute coverage of the war, it was also inundated with critiques of the coverage and countless analyses of the factors motivating U.S. involvement. Being able to sort through the plethora of opinions accompanying today's major issues, and to draw one's own conclusions, can be a complicated and frustrating struggle. It is the editors' hope that Current Controversies will help readers with this struggle.

Introduction

"Few academics doubt that protecting biodiversity will be one of the most serious challenges facing humankind during the 21st century."

Biodiversity is a term that is short for biological diversity—the great variety and richness of plant, animal, fungi, and microbial life forms that exist on Earth. As of 2008, approximately 1.7 million different species of animals, plants, fungi, and lichens have been discovered and named by biologists, but the true number of life forms on the planet may be much larger, perhaps ten million or more, if all bacteria and fungi species are counted. There also is great genetic variation within many of the planet's species. In addition, the Earth contains a diverse number of ecosystems, or natural habitats, to support the many complex varieties of life.

Scientists today agree that biodiversity on all these levels is vital for the health of the planet and the continuation of human life. The human race literally depends on plants and animals for food, clothing, shelter, medicines, and many other necessities and products. Biodiversity is also required to purify the air and water, regulate climates, control erosion, and provide the very oxygen that humans and animal species breathe. Of course, no one can imagine living in a world that does not provide the spectacular scenery, natural abundance, and beauty currently found on the globe.

Yet the scientific community is also in agreement that the Earth's biodiversity is rapidly being lost. According to the 2006 Red List of Threatened Species, a highly respected inventory published by the International Union for the Conservation of Nature and Natural Resources (IUCN), out of a total list of about 42,000 species evaluated since 1963, 784 species have been officially recorded as extinct and more than 16,000 species are threatened with extinction. This list of threatened species includes approximately 12 percent of bird species, 23 percent of mammals, and 32 percent of amphibians, as well as a large number of plant species. Most biologists, however, think the real number of possible extinctions is much higher. In fact, some scientists predict that up to 50 percent of all the Earth's species may be lost within the coming century.

The reasons for the dramatic rates of biodiversity loss are also quite clear to scientists and others in the academic world. The rapid growth of the human population—from 1.75 billion in 1900 to more than 6 billion as of 2008—is stretching the planet's resources to the limit. Human activities such as farming, hunting, fishing, and logging are eating away at natural habitats along with urban sprawl—the spread of homes and businesses into the rural lands around cities. Moreover, in many places, human travel has allowed exotic and invasive plant and animal species to overwhelm native species. Meanwhile, the by-products of the industrial and fossil fuel age, including water, air, and soil pollution, have permeated even remote regions of the globe and are believed to be causing the global warming trend that is changing the world's climates. And with the world's population continuing to rise at a rate of almost a billion births each year, these pressures on the environment are only expected to increase. Many scientists agree that these factors are causing a biodiversity crisis, and many think that it could be as serious as the one that caused the extinction of the dinosaurs and many other creatures millions of years ago. Indeed, few academics doubt that protecting biodiversity will be one of the most serious challenges facing humankind during the 21st century.

Some scientists, however, dispute the claim that today's biodiversity losses will be catastrophic. These biologists see extinction as a natural process and suggest that many of the species being lost are not necessary for major ecosystems to survive. Although there is clear evidence that greater diversity helps make ecosystems more resilient to pressures from pollution and other threats, no one really knows at this point exactly how much diversity is needed to prevent a widespread collapse that could threaten human existence. Yet conservationists worry that waiting for more definitive science on this issue could delay action until it is too late to prevent a true catastrophe.

There is also disagreement about how best to protect biodiversity. Many environmentalists believe that the only solution is for governments to place restrictions on the types of human activities that harm natural habitats, but these types of solutions are likely to slow or prevent economic development and cause higher prices for goods and services—costs that policymakers are often reluctant to embrace. In 1992, 157 nations signed an international treaty called the Convention on Biological Diversity, designed to encourage a coordinated global response to biodiversity losses and promote more sustainable economic development, but as of 2008 little meaningful action had been taken to stop or slow down the species and habitat declines.

The overall position taken in the literature on biodiversity loss is that it is an urgent problem that requires people to make decisions and take action during the early decades of the twenty-first century. These responses to biodiversity issues can determine the quality of life for the next generation and possibly the very fate of the planet. Biologist Peter J. Bryant makes this point in his book, *Biodiversity and Conservation*:

> Our generation is the first one that really became aware of the fact that the human population is causing irreparable damage to the planet ... [and] ours is the only generation that can prevent a massive loss of biological diversity. Huge losses have already taken place and we will have to make

major changes in the way we treat the planet if we are to save it in anything like an intact state.

The contributors to *Current Controversies: Biodiversity* provide various perspectives on the nature and extent of the problem of biodiversity loss, its causes, and possible solutions.

CHAPTER 1

Is Biodiversity Loss a Serious Problem?

Biodiversity: An Overview

Environmental Literacy Council

The independent, nonprofit Environmental Literacy Council gives teachers the tools to help students develop environmental literacy: a fundamental understanding of the systems of the world, both living and non-living, along with the analytical skills needed to weigh scientific evidence and policy choices.

Why is biological diversity important? Many arguments can be made from scientific, philosophical, economic, ethical, and aesthetic perspectives. Scientists argue that much remains to be learned about many species and ecosystems around the world and that the loss of these species would foreclose that opportunity. Certain rare species are singled out as worth saving for their sake; the loss of the Sumatran tiger, for example, or the rhinocerous would be mourned by many who have never seen these animals in the wild. There is great beauty in forests, coral reefs, savannahs, and other landscapes that is worth preserving for future generations, as well as our own, to appreciate.

Natural resources also provide critical ecosystem services. Forests retain moisture in the soil and prevent erosion; hillside areas can be subject to mudslides where forests are cleared, resulting in loss of life and property. Of the approximately 1.4 million species that are known, almost one million are insects and other invertebrates, and these are, as E.O. Wilson has said, "the little things that run the world" by breaking down plant and animal matter and making it available as nutrients. Crop and forest lands provide food and wood for shelter and sustenance. The interactions between the living and the non-living parts of the environment provide essential ecosystems services of soil formation, climate control, and water recycling. In one

Environmental Literacy Council, "Value of Biodiversity," *www.enviroliteracy.org*, October 31, 2007. Reproduced by permission.

study, published in 1997 in the science journal *Nature*, researchers estimated the value of these ecosystem services at between $16 trillion and $54 trillion a year.

Arguments for increased international efforts to conserve habitats and ecosystems often emphasize the value of biodiversity to humans: the "un-mined riches" that we may discover in plants and animals and the potential of new food sources. For example, approximately 25 percent of all prescription drugs in the United States are derived from plants. The rosy periwinkle from Madagascar is the source of a drug used in the treatment of Hodgkin's disease and leukemia. The Pacific yew tree is the source of Taxol, a drug which has been found effective in treatment of ovarian cancer. Some drugs found have been identified through native folklore. Peruvian Indians, for example, treated malaria with an extract from the bark of the Cinchona tree. Study of this extract led to discovery and use of quinine. the first effective treatment for malaria.

The potential for discovering medicines is often cited as an argument for international cooperation in preserving tropical forests, but also as a means for doing so, by finding useful products that can be extracted profitably from the plants and animals of the rainforest, through bioprospecting. For example, Glaxo Wellcome, a British pharmaceutical company, funds the Centre for Natural Products Research in Singapore, which surveys species in Asia for medicinal purposes. Conservation International has initiated an agreement between Bristol-Meyers Squib, Suriname, and the National Institutes of Health.

There are concerns about bioprospecting, however. Some developing countries maintain that they will not receive a sufficient portion of the profits from drugs developed from plants found within their borders. On the other hand, the costs of isolating useful species, developing drugs and other products, and testing them for use is enormously expensive, and those costs are borne by the drug companies.

The Earth Is on the Verge of a Global Biodiversity Catastrophe

Steve Connor

Steve Connor is the science editor of The Independent, *a British newspaper.*

Life on earth is facing a major crisis with thousands of species threatened with imminent extinction—a global emergency demanding urgent action. This is the view of 19 of the world's most eminent biodiversity specialists, who have called on governments to establish a political framework to save the planet.

A Call for Action

The planet is losing species faster than at any time since 65 million years ago, when the earth was hit by an enormous asteroid that wiped out thousands of animals and plants, including the dinosaurs. Scientists estimate that the current rate at which species are becoming extinct is between 100 and 1,000 times greater than the normal "background" extinction rate—and say this is all due to human activity.

The call for action comes from some of the most distinguished scientists in the field, such as Georgina Mace of the UK Institute of Zoology; Peter Raven, the head of the Missouri Botanical Garden in St Louis, and Robert Watson, chief scientist at the World Bank. "For the sake of the planet, the biodiversity science community had to create a way to get organised, to co-ordinate its work across disciplines and together, with one clear voice, advise governments on steps to halt the potentially catastrophic loss of species already occurring," Dr Watson said.

Scientists estimate that 12 per cent of all birds, 23 per cent of mammals, . . . [and] a third of amphibians . . . are threatened with imminent extinction.

In a joint declaration, published . . . [July 20, 2006] in *Nature*, the scientists say that the earth is on the verge of a biodiversity catastrophe and that only a global political initiative stands a chance of stemming the loss. They say: "There is growing recognition that the diversity of life on earth, including the variety of genes, species and ecosystems, is an irreplaceable natural heritage crucial to human well-being and sustainable development. There is also clear scientific evidence that we are on the verge of a major biodiversity crisis. Virtually all aspects of biodiversity are in steep decline and a large number of populations and species are likely to become extinct this century." "Despite this evidence, biodiversity is still consistently undervalued and given inadequate weight in both private and public decisions. There is an urgent need to bridge the gap between science and policy by creating an international body of biodiversity experts," they say.

An Unprecedented Loss of Diversity

More than a decade ago, Edward O. Wilson, the Harvard naturalist, first estimated that about 30,000 species were going extinct each year—an extinction rate of about three an hour. Further research has confirmed that just about every group of animals and plants—from mosses and ferns to palm trees, frogs, and monkeys—is experiencing an unprecedented loss of diversity.

Scientists estimate that 12 per cent of all birds, 23 per cent of mammals, a quarter of conifers, a third of amphibians and more than half of all palm trees are threatened with imminent extinction. Climate change alone could lead to the further extinction of between 15 and 37 per cent of all species by the end of the century. The scientists say: "Because biodiversity loss is essentially irreversible, it poses serious threats to sustainable development and the quality of life of future generations."

There have been five previous mass extinctions in the 3.5 billion-year history of life on earth. All are believed to have been caused by major geophysical events that halted photosynthesis, such as an asteroid collision or the mass eruption of supervolcanoes. The present "sixth wave" of extinction began with the migration of modern humans out of Africa about 100,000 years ago. It accelerated with the invention of agriculture 10,000 years ago and began to worsen with the development of industry in the 18th century.

The scientists believe that a body similar to the Intergovernmental Panel on Climate Change could help governments . . . tackle the continuing loss of species.

Anne Larigauderie, executive director of Diversitas, a Paris-based conservation group, said that the situation was now so grave that an international body with direct links with global leaders was essential. "The point is to establish an international mechanism that will provide regular and independent scientific advice on biodiversity," Dr Larigauderie said. "We know that extinction is a natural phenomenon but the rate of extinction is now between 100 and 1,000 times higher than the background rate. It is an unprecedented loss."

The scientists believe that a body similar to the Intergovernmental Panel on Climate Change could help governments to tackle the continuing loss of species. "Biodiversity is much more than counting species. It's crucial to the functioning of the planet and the loss of species is extremely serious," Dr Larigauderie said. "Everywhere we look, we are losing the fabric of life. It's a major crisis."

Species Under Threat

Land mammals: The first comprehensive inventory of land mammals in 1996 found a quarter, including the Iberian lynx, were in danger of extinction. The situation has worsened since.

Reptiles and amphibians: The Chinese alligator is the most endangered crocodilian—a survey in 1999 found just 150. Frogs, toads, newts and salamanders are the most threatened land vertebrates.

Birds: One in five species are believed to be in danger of extinction; that amounts to about 2,000 of the 9,775 named species. Most are at risk from logging, intensive agriculture, trapping and habitat encroachment. Many experts believe the Philippine eagle and wandering albatross could become extinct this century.

Marine life: The oceans were thought to be immune from the activities of man on land, but this is no longer true. Pollution, overfishing, loss of marine habitats and global warming have a dramatic impact on biological diversity. More than 100 species of fish, including the basking shark, are on the red list of threatened species.

Plants: Many plants have yet to be formally described, classified and named—and some are being lost before they have been discovered by scientists. Plants of every type are being lost.

Insects and invertebrates: Many insects are wiped out by pesticide-reliant intensive agriculture. Others, such as the partula tree snails of Tahiti, are menaced by invasive species.

Biodiversity Is Essential to Every Aspect of Human Life

U.S. Agency for International Development

The U.S. Agency for International Development is a federal agency that provides assistance to countries recovering from disaster, trying to escape poverty, and engaging in democratic reforms.

Biodiversity is the variety and variability of life on Earth. This includes all of the plants and animals that live and grow on the Earth, all of the habitats that they call home, and all of the natural processes of which they are a part. The earth supports an incredible array of biodiversity—from Thailand's tiny bumblebee bat to the ocean's great blue whale—with plants and animals of all shapes and sizes in between. This fantastic variety of life is found in diverse habitats ranging from the hottest desert to tropical rainforests to the arctic tundra. Biodiversity is essential to every aspect of the way that humans live around the world. Plants and animals provide people with food and medicine, trees play an important role in absorbing greenhouse gases and cleaning the air we breathe, and rivers and watersheds provide the clean water that we drink.

Unfortunately, the earth's biodiversity is disappearing, with an estimated 1,000 species per year becoming extinct. Conserving biodiversity is especially crucial in developing countries where people's livelihoods are directly dependent on natural resources such as forests, fisheries and wildlife.

USAID's Efforts to Save Biodiversity

In recognition of the importance of biodiversity, USAID has made biodiversity conservation a key goal under its program to protect the environment. USAID is supporting conserva-

U.S. Agency for International Development, "Environment: Biodiversity," *USAID.gov*, February 28, 2007.

tion activities in more than 50 countries, seeking to maintain the variety of species and the habitats in which they occur.

Biodiversity is the very foundation for all the Earth's essential goods and services.

USAID is working with communities, non-governmental organizations, and governments to develop environmental policies and management practices that conserve biodiversity and, at the same time, sustain local livelihoods. This can involve empowering communities to become stronger actors in the management of resources. USAID also invests in building the capacity of foreign governments, non-governmental organizations and communities to better manage protected areas. In addition, USAID is promoting enterprise-based conservation initiatives (such as eco-tourism), which provide economic benefits from the preservation of biological resources. To complement these activities, USAID fosters greater public awareness of conservation issues by supporting the development of outreach and environmental education programs.

Why Conserve Biodiversity?

Biodiversity is the very foundation for all the Earth's essential goods and services. The air we breathe, water we drink, and the food we eat all depend on the Earth's rich biodiversity. USAID's biodiversity conservation activities not only protect the environment in developing countries but also have significant economic value to the United States.

Plants and animals provide people with food and medicine. Forty percent of all prescriptions written today are composed from the natural compounds found in different species. An estimated 80,000 edible plants are found in the world, and one in every three mouthfuls of the food you swallow is prepared from plants pollinated by wild insects and animals. The extinction of each additional species results in the irreversible loss of unique genetic materials, each of which has potential for development of medicines and foods and associated enterprises that create jobs.

The net economic benefits of biodiversity are estimated to be at least $3 trillion per year, or 11 percent of the annual world economic output.

While plants and animals keep you well fed and healthy, trees play an important role in absorbing greenhouse gases. Through photosynthesis, trees absorb and store atmospheric carbon, helping to combat global warming and purifying the air we breathe. Forests also control soil erosion and purify water.

As natural systems break down, people around the world are forced to find alternative and often more costly ways to maintain adequate supplies of clean water or to deal with increasingly polluted air. The net economic benefits of biodiversity are estimated to be at least $3 trillion per year, or 11 percent of the annual world economic output.

Biodiversity Is Important to Medicine, Bioengineering, and Health Care

Julie Majeres

Julie Majeres is a fellow in environmental studies at the Pacific Research Institute, a nonprofit organization located in San Francisco, California, that advocates for personal responsibility and individual liberty in national and state issues.

For many of the more than 190,000 women who will be diagnosed with breast cancer this year, the drug Taxol could be what saves their lives. The active ingredient in Taxol, termed one of the "miracle drugs" of the past 10 years, was originally isolated from the Pacific yew tree.

"Thanks in large part to medicines developed in the past decade, cancer deaths are on the decline," said Alan Holmer, president of Pharmaceutical Research and Manufacturers of America (PhRMA). Still, one out of every four Americans will die from cancer, which remains the second leading cause of death by disease.

Biodiversity and Medicines

The No. 1 weapon against cancer today has come to be pharmaceuticals, which are often developed through research on biochemicals found in wild plants and animals. The industry had revenues of $359 billion in 2000, as much as $180 billion of which came from products developed from living things. According to a recent study by the UN [United Nations] Environment Program (UNEP), however, one potentially lifesaving drug is lost every two years as a result of plant extinction.

Julie Majeres, "The Politics of Biodiversity," *World and I*, vol. 17, iss. 12, December 2002, p. 54. Copyright © 2002 News World Communications, Inc. Reproduced by permission.

Thus, biodiversity loss could have a big impact on medicine, bioengineering, and health care in the United States and other Western countries promising to make it one of the more serious environmental—and ultimately political—issues of this century. Why? Because wealthy nations want access to potentially drug-rich biodiversity, and the greatest diversity of organisms is found in an equatorial belt of relatively poor countries in which poverty, war, and corruption are apparently contributing to the extinction of plant and animal species. A hopeful recent trend is the emergence of a movement by private-sector philanthropic groups to aggressively conserve targeted tropical areas.

With the human population rising worldwide, the battle promises to get worse before it gets better.

The problem of biodiversity loss is illustrated in Brazil, where vast stretches of rain forest teeming with plants and animals, many as yet unknown to science, are being cleared by poverty-stricken homesteaders, who farm for a few years and then abandon the exhausted soil. Another example is Liberia, in which the West African tropical forest has shrunk before an onslaught of illegal lumbering that has financed the barbarous Revolutionary United Front rebel group in next-door Sierra Leone. In the United States, government and corporations have improved air and water quality and greatly reduced the concentration of toxins in the environment, but efforts to protect endangered species have been less successful.

With the human population rising worldwide, the battle promises to get worse before it gets better. Still, there are reasons for optimism. One is a proposal to spend $30 billion to purchase and protect a slew of rain-forest tracts that contain the world's greatest biodiversity concentrations.

Why We Should Care

Some might reasonably ask why we should worry about the loss of species as a result of human activity, especially when more than 99 percent of all species that have ever come into existence have become extinct. What is the point of trying to prevent what may be inevitable?

Scientists and environmentalists contend that we should care because all species—in addition to their potential medical value—provide scientific, economic, and recreational benefits. Harrison Ford, a longtime Conservation International board member, tells us we should worry because "plants and animals provide food and medicine, clean our air and water, and keep our planet alive."

It would be well for the human community to do all it can to avert a sixth catastrophic event, which would drastically affect the growing human population.

As a PhRMA report, "The Value of Medicines," indicates, drugs "help people—and the health care system—avoid disability, surgery, hospitalization, and nursing home care, often decreasing the total cost of caring for an illness." In addition, according to the U.S. Department of Agriculture, finding new plants is crucial for improving farming, because they can be bred with existing domesticated varieties to make crops "more productive, nutritious, durable, or simply better tasting."

Many environmentalists and scientists contend that these benefits provided by Mother Nature are but a few reasons for concern over the loss of biodiversity. It's a concern that will only increase as the human population continues to grow, peaking at an expected 9–10 billion people in the late twenty-first century.

But biologists sharply disagree over the severity of the biodiversity-loss problem. The most extreme warn that 20 percent of all tropical species will go extinct by 2022 and 50 percent by 2042. Others predict a much smaller figure—less than 1 percent by 2050. They expect the extinction rate to decline as human population growth decelerates and biodiversity protection becomes more affordable and successful. However, some scientists predict a sixth mass worldwide extinction, similar to what occurred when the dinosaurs disappeared 65 million years ago.

The current approach ... is simply to make lists of threatened animals and plants and then try to protect them.

All previous mass extinctions resulted from climate change or some global catastrophe, such as a huge meteor striking Earth. Although biodiversity has actually increased throughout the planet's history, it would be well for the human community to do all it can to avert a sixth catastrophic event, which would drastically affect the growing human population through species loss. If we are to avert disaster, what exactly should we save, and how do we achieve success with limited capital?

What Has Been Done

The current approach in the United States and around the world is simply to make lists of threatened animals and plants and then try to protect them. U.S. policy is embodied in the controversial Endangered Species Act (ESA). Unlike the Clean Air and Clean Water Acts, the ESA does little more than maintain lists while establishing modest policy—while provoking hardworking landowners whose private property all too often comes under the statute's regulations.

Of the 1,259 threatened and endangered species listed for the United States, only 13 have been delisted because they recovered, while 7 apparently became extinct. These poor results have added fuel to the fires of accusation and outrage. They stand as evidence of the urgent need to establish better methods of assessing and monitoring biodiversity. They also show that little can be done unless private landowners—environmental stewards of roughly 80 percent of American land—are given proper incentives to protect species.

The rest of the world has fared only slightly better. The global list used by the United Nations is the World Conservation Union's Red List, which has completely assessed the world's mammals and birds but only a fraction of the plants, invertebrates, fish, reptiles, and amphibians. The 2000 Red List reported 11,046 species threatened with extinction. Though this number represents only 0.6 percent of all known species, it includes 24 percent of all mammals and 12 percent of birds. The Red List goes a step further than the ESA, identifying the ways in which critical habitats are threatened, such as habitat loss, exploitation, or natural disasters. The data show that the primary threat to biodiversity is habitat degradation. This knowledge is spurring a shift in public conservation policy from protection of individual species to conservation of entire ecosystems.

To protect animal and plant diversity, we need to know how many organisms there actually are on Earth.

To date, however, there has been no worldwide or even U.S. consensus on which system is best—not even agreement on what scale should be used (global or local). To illustrate the difficulty of whether to use a global or local approach to species conservation, take the example of the grizzly bear. It once roamed as far south as Texas but has become locally extinct in many states; nonetheless, it is far from extinct globally.

The United Nations states in its "Global Environment Outlook-3" report, "Much of the relevant information on the status of species is qualitative or anecdotal, and it is therefore difficult to develop a quantitative overview of global trends." It is precisely this lack of agreement on any verifiable data that makes biodiversity so contentious an issue, because the true costs of species extinction are difficult to estimate in proportion to other important social goals.

Private Sector to the Rescue

The shift in policy toward ecosystem conservation has added weight to some new ideas. In his latest book, *The Future of Life*, biologist Edward Wilson makes a dozen policy recommendations, one of which has received considerable public attention. Wilson asks conservationists to rescue 25 special ecosystems, called "hot spots," that cover 1.4 percent of the world's land surface and contain the largest concentration of biodiversity.

He estimates the price tag for such an endeavor to be $30 billion. This may seem like chump change compared to the gross world product of about $30 trillion, but measured against the annual budgets of the U.S. Department of the Interior ($13 billion) or UNEP ($3.9 million), the number is formidable. Because governments have done so little on this issue, the private sector has become by comparison quite prominent. Along the way, the task of raising the money and protecting the hot spots has developed some unexpected relationships.

These ties are so strange that ABC's Robert Krulwich expressed surprise that Conservation International (CI) is "run by the cement king of Mexico; the head of British Petroleum, a giant oil company; the chief of a Filipino power conglomerate; a computer billionaire from California," and actor Harrison Ford. The Gordon and Betty Moore Foundation (Gordon Moore is chairman of CI's board and founder of Intel Corporation) gave the organization a quarter of a billion dollars to jump-start the hot spots conservation effort.

CI is not alone in its efforts. The Nature Conservancy (TNC), the revenues of which last year topped all environmental organizations at $546 million, has started a "One Billion Dollar Campaign," the largest private conservation campaign ever undertaken, to conserve 200 spots. In addition, all the top environmental organizations work in some way to conserve biodiversity.

Private conservation efforts have long taken the lead in forging partnerships at the community level and protecting biodiversity on an international scale. These efforts initiated the shift toward ecosystem protection long before governments prompted such policy changes. TNC alone boasts having almost 13 million acres privately protected in the United States and more than 80 million acres abroad.

[One day] perhaps ... humankind will "subdue" the Earth by husbanding it wisely and well.

Private entities are also a step ahead of government in fostering incentives for landowners to protect endangered species and habitat. They are achieving successes that would be too costly for government bureaucracies. The task is accomplished one local problem at a time, working with farmers, ranchers, governments, and industry. Take, for example, the gray wolf compensation program started by Hank Fischer of [the environment group] Defenders of Wildlife. The number of wolves in Yellowstone National Park and Idaho has grown from zero to more than 400 since 1995. It could not have been accomplished without the $175,000 that Defenders paid ranchers to compensate for livestock losses. Before, ranchers would have implemented the "shoot, shovel, and shut up" method of ridding their land of wolves. As former National Park Service director William Penn Mott states, "It's economics that makes ranchers hate wolves. Pay them for their losses, and the controversy will subside." The program has been so successful that Defenders has started a similar grizzly bear compensation program.

A United Effort

Although biodiversity remains a controversial issue, there is reason for hope as corporations, individuals, and organizations are uniting in an effort to transcend conflict.

Can humans and other species continue to coexist and flourish together? Majority opinion tends to be cautiously optimistic. Advances in science and technology are the only means to ensure that humanity will reach its population peak with continued declines in poverty and hunger, steady increases in wealth across the globe, and sustained biodiversity protection.

To protect animal and plant diversity, we need to know how many organisms there actually are on Earth. After all, we can't know if we are succeeding in protecting, say, a particular plant unless we know that it exists and whether it's threatened by human encroachment. So we need to accelerate the cataloging of organisms the world over—especially in the tropical regions, where there is the greatest biodiversity. Today's computer information systems make it possible to map all habitat, ecosystem, and species locations and analyze them as never before.

Once the complete "endangered" list is in place, then scientific expertise and private-sector conservation organizations can come into play, perhaps leading to the day when humankind will "subdue" the Earth by husbanding it wisely and well.

Marine Biodiversity Is Just as Important as Land Diversity

The Economist

The Economist is a British news magazine that covers world business, current affairs, finance, science, and technology matters.

Everybody knows that global fish stocks are heading for collapse. That is why governments try to limit the amount of fish taken out of the sea. But recent research suggests that the world is going about regulating fishing the wrong way—that fish stocks would fare better if efforts were made to protect entire ecosystems rather than individual species.

The Importance of Marine Diversity

There are plenty of data to prove the importance of diversity on dry land. Until recently [as of 2006], however, there was little evidence that the same was the case in the oceans, which make up 90% of the biosphere, and on which a billion people rely for their livelihoods.

In order to establish whether diversity matters in the sea as well as on land, 11 marine biologists, along with three economists, have spent the past three years crunching all the numbers they could lay their hands on. These ranged from the current United Nations Food and Agriculture Organisation's database to information hundreds of years old, gleaned from kitchen records and archaeology. The results of their comprehensive analysis have been published in *Science*.

Marine biodiversity, they report, matters because it is variety per se that delivers services—such as maintaining water quality and processing nutrients—to humans as well as the

The Economist, "Every Little Fish; Marine Biodiversity," vol. 381, iss. 8502, November 4, 2006, p. 89. Copyright © 2006 Economist Newspaper Ltd. Republished with permission of Economist Newspaper Ltd., conveyed through Copyright Clearance Center, Inc.

goods people reap from the sea. It also ensures these goods and services recover relatively rapidly after an accident or natural disturbance. The new work is silent on exactly how biodiversity protects these things—merely showing that it does. Earlier work though has shown some possible mechanisms. One example from a study in Jamaica showed that continuously removing algae-grazers from a reef allowed the algae to overwhelm the coral.

The more species an ocean region has, the more robustly it seems to cope with overexploitation.

The latest study, led by Boris Worm of Dalhousie University, in Halifax, Canada, gathered the available material into four separate groups. The researchers found the same result from different pools of data, in different types of marine ecosystems and at different scales.

The Data on Marine Diversity

In the first the marine ecologists re-examined 32 small-scale experiments in which researchers had altered the variety of sea life and recorded what happened. Overall, each of the six ecosystem processes examined—which included the maintenance of stability and improved water quality—worked better when there were more species than when there were fewer.

This is not as obvious as it may seem. Until now, some scientists have thought that many individuals of the same species with certain talents could perform specific tasks better than the same number of individuals from different species. For example, one type of seagrass may process nutrients more effectively than other types, so a bed devoted entirely to the talented seagrass might be expected to conduct this processing better than a mixed area. The research suggests this is not so.

Second, Dr. Worm considered estuaries. Marine extinctions are uncovered slowly on a global scale, but local disappearances are much more rapidly apparent. They collected long-term historical records from 12 coastal areas in Europe and North America, including information on the Roman elimination of the Dalmatian pelican from the Wadden Sea and the removal of the Atlantic sturgeon from the Chesapeake Bay and the Delaware Bay.

Analysing these data revealed that estuaries and coastlines are less able to maintain, for example, water quality, as the number of species found within them declines. Going back over several centuries, when biodiversity falls, people desert the beaches, coastlines become more liable to flooding and blooms of algae are more likely to gain a footing.

The way things are going, commercial fish stocks will collapse completely by 2048.

That theory was tested on a third group of data—records kept by the United Nations from 1950 to 2003 of the fish and invertebrates caught in large expanses of the ocean all around the world. These data make up 83% of all records of all catches of fish over the past half-century. Dr. Worm and his colleagues discovered that the more species an ocean region has, the more robustly it seems to cope with overexploitation.

Preserve Ecosystems, Not Individual Species

The findings suggest that governments should rethink the way they try to manage fisheries. Marine reserves are common in the tropics, but policymakers in temperate countries tend to focus on one species at a time to control numbers of that species caught. They might do better to spend more time thinking about ecosystems and less haggling over quotas.

Some governments claim to have already come around to the idea. In America, Britain, and Canada officials are considering how to redraft fisheries policy. Scientists hope that the move will push the inevitably unhappy compromise between their recommendations and fishermen's aspirations closer to their way.

Dr. Worm's fourth analysis showed that the damage could be reversed. In it, he pooled data from areas where fishing had been banned, either because stocks had collapsed or because the space had been designated as a marine reserve. These included the Georges Bank off the east coast of America and Canada, where disastrous overfishing for cod threatened the collapse of stocks.

On average, the number of species in the 44 sites increased by 23%. In the areas around the protected regions fishermen reported catching, on average, four times as many fish per trip as previously. The researchers also examined whether the recovery was sufficient to make the protected areas more resilient to storms and changes in temperature, but the results were not statistically significant.

Dr. Worm reckons that, the way things are going, commercial fish stocks will collapse completely by 2048. The date may be spuriously precise, but the danger is there. And so, if Dr. Worm is right, is a better way of making sure that it doesn't happen.

Scientific Study of Biodiversity Decline Is Still in the Early Stages

Shahid Naeem

Shahid Naeem is an expert in biodiversity research and chairman of Columbia University's Ecology, Evolution, and Environmental Biology Department.

Do ecosystems require a rich diversity of species in order to remain healthy? The question is important for policymakers, as a positive answer would mean that the conservation of biodiversity, and in particular the protection of a high number of different species, should be a high priority for all those concerned with maintaining healthy ecosystems.

Just how much biodiversity is needed to ensure that ecosystems are healthy and life sustaining, is still the subject of considerable [scientific] debate.

The UN Convention on Biological Diversity declares that biodiversity—the biological and ecological diversity of plants, animals, and microbes—is important "for maintaining life-sustaining systems". This statement is based on the observation that areas of land that are rich in clean water, fertile soils and productive forests are also rich in species. It follows that their degraded counterparts—polluted, infertile and unproductive areas of land—generally have a relatively low number of species. In other words, that biodiversity must be an integral component of life-sustaining systems.

But does biodiversity itself lead to clean water, fertile soils and productive forests? Or does it simply flourish under such

Shahid Naeem, "How Biodiversity Loss Affects the Health of Ecosystems," *Science and Development Network*, February 2004. www.scidev.net. Reproduced by permission.

conditions? To put it another way, is the loss of biodiversity simply a symptom of unhealthy ecosystems? Or is it this loss that causes ecosystems to be unhealthy?

Since the Convention was signed in 1992, ecologists and environmental researchers have become deeply divided over the issue. A consensus, however, has gradually emerged: researchers now agree that a well-functioning ecosystem capable of sustaining life does indeed require a high level of biodiversity.

Precisely what those levels are, however, or just how much biodiversity is needed to ensure that ecosystems are healthy and life sustaining, is still the subject of considerable debate in the ecological community. Its outcome has important implications for the policymakers who are seeking to devise and justify policies aimed at preserving the complex web of ecosystems that support life on earth.

Why Are Ecosystems Important?

The word 'ecosystem' is a contraction of 'ecological system', and refers to the way that nature can be viewed as a system or, according to the *Merriam-Webster Dictionary*, a "regularly interacting or interdependent group of items forming a unified whole". A forest is an example of an ecosystem, as is a river delta.

The healthy functioning of the global ecosystem, and the individual ecosystems that make it up, are essential for the well-being of humanity.

A wide range of the benefits of nature are attributable to the workings of ecosystems. They include soil fertility, soil retention, water quality, food production, the degradation of pollutants, flood regulation, pollination and the regulation of insect pest populations by natural predators such as spiders and wasps.

Some ecological economists have even tried to put a financial value on such 'economic services'. Robert Costanza and colleagues at the Institute for Ecological Economics at the University of Maryland, United States, for example, have placed the global figure at between US$17 trillion and US$54 trillion (at 1994 rates), suggesting that the value is the same order of magnitude as the world's economic output.

But we hardly need economists to tell us that the healthy functioning of the global ecosystem, and the individual ecosystems that make it up, are essential for the well-being of humanity. And that makes it all the more important to understand the role that biodiversity plays in the way ecosystems operate.

Research into Biodiversity and Ecosystems: What We Have Learned

There are between 10 million and 100 million species on the Earth. Most ecosystems contain hundreds to thousands of species. For any one ecosystem, these species can be divided into one of three so-called 'functional groups', based on whether they *produce, consume* or *decompose* organic matter, the source of energy for living organisms.

Every working ecosystem needs at least one species from each of these functional groups if it is to process energy effectively. But is it sufficient for an ecosystem to have just one species from each group (for example, a plant, a herbivore and a decomposer, such as a bacterium)? Or does a healthy, functioning ecosystem require all of the hundreds to thousands of species that we typically find?

This question is similar to asking whether a computer needs all the parts that we see when we take off its cover. One basic approach, which can apply either to ecosystems or computers, is to divide each into its many component parts and then put them all together again in various configurations in order to see what happens. Such a process has a number of functions. It helps us to understand how the parts relate to one another, to identify how they each help the overall system to work, and to establish which components are more important.

Several laboratory and field-based biodiversity experiments have used this approach. Much of this research has focused on the behaviour of systems made up of plants, which are easiest to manipulate. But there are an increasing number of studies of systems that include animals, microbes and even combinations of all three types of organism.

Three Ecosystem Models

One of the goals of such research is to compare the relative claims of three different models that explain the relationship between species and ecosystems. The first of these is the 'redundancy model', which postulates that the actual number of individual species is less important to a working ecosystem than the presence of all functional groups.

Such an approach predicts that if a functional group loses a species, other species within that group will increase in number to take its place. For example, if the number of wildebeest decreases, other members of the herbivore functional group will increase in number. This hypothesis therefore suggests that species-poor versions of ecosystems should work just as well as their species-rich counterparts, provided that an appropriate combination of functional groups always exists.

The second model, known as the 'idiosyncratic model', maintains that although the number of species *does* affect how an ecosystem works, the way in which this happens is unpredictable. This model is based on the idea that if you remove species from a complex ecosystem, it is impossible to predict what will happen; the system may work better, get worse, or show no change at all.

It is already known, for example, that in certain ecosystems, there are species—known as 'keystone' species—whose loss dramatically alters the ecosystem's properties. Other ecosystems, however, are known to have lost species without showing any change.

Changes in biodiversity can affect how an ecosystem works, and . . . while some of these impacts can be predicted, others cannot.

Finally, the 'complementarity model' says that the number of species does play an important role in the way an ecosystem works, as different species contribute to ecosystems in complementary ways. Plants with shallow and deep roots, for example, produce more biomass when they grow together than either plant can produce alone. Complementary species are therefore more effective in using resources, which implies that ecosystems work better when such species are present.

The First Experiment on Biodiversity and Ecosystems

The first experiment designed to examine these three models was carried out at Imperial College London, in the early 1990s. Sixteen terrestrial ecosystems were housed in identical chambers, each occupying an area of one square metre. Each chamber had exactly the same amount of soil, water, light and rainfall. The only variable was the level of biodiversity, with chambers containing varying numbers of plant and animal (earthworms, insects, molluscs and other invertebrates) species. The researchers also separately planted a number of random combinations of the plants that were used in the main experiment.

This trial was the first to demonstrate that even if all environmental factors are held as constant as possible, simply changing biodiversity is sufficient to significantly alter ecosystem functioning. For the researchers found that varying the quantity and mix of species did indeed affect key ecosystem functions, including carbon dioxide flux, plant production, and soil nutrient and water retention.

Furthermore, although not all ecosystem functions showed the same kind of response, the data collected on carbon dioxide flux and plant production best fitted the complementarity model—namely, that a loss of species led to reductions in ecosystem processes due to fewer synergies between the different species.

An Emerging Consensus—and Points of Disagreement

Since those first experiments were published, dozens of experimental and theoretical studies have been performed around the world. Perhaps the most significant have been the grassland biodiversity experiments carried out by David Tilman and colleagues at the University of Minnesota, as well as the BIODEPTH grassland experiments in Europe led by Andy Hector (formerly of Imperial College London) and colleagues. These have confirmed that the positive effects of biodiversity observed initially under small-scale conditions are also seen when using a much larger variety of species, and conducted over much larger scales.

Functional diversity is a measure of how an individual species contributes to the workings of an ecosystem.

Additional studies have examined how ecosystems are affected by diversity in aquatic insects, microbes, zooplankton, wetland plant species and soil fauna, for example. These improved upon the original experimental design, using more combinations and types of species, working outdoors under more natural conditions, using larger plots, conducting experiments for longer periods, and using an increasingly complex and sophisticated array of analytical methods.

Their findings have been mixed. Some have shown that changes in biodiversity could significantly affect the workings of ecosystems. Others have shown no significant response. As a result, drawing overall conclusions from the results has not been easy. Nevertheless, a consensus is beginning to emerge along the following lines of argument:

- First, that history, geography and local climate are the primary factors governing how an ecosystem performs; biodiversity plays an important—but secondary—role.

- Secondly, that changes in biodiversity—such as the loss of dominant or 'keystone' species, the loss or addition of complementary species, or the addition of invasive species—can affect how an ecosystem works, and that while some of these impacts can be predicted, others cannot.

- Finally, that disruption to an ecosystem can often be reduced by maintaining biodiversity as closely as possible to its historical levels.

This consensus contains elements of each of the three original models—namely redundancy, idiosyncrasy and complementarity.

Moving Beyond Numbers

If biodiversity matters to the environment, as the experience described above appears to confirm, what are the implications for policy, management and conservation?

Researchers and policymakers who deal with biodiversity issues are primarily concerned with cataloguing, and subsequently conserving, individual species. These are often found in what are called biodiversity hotspots and other areas where species diversity is high. Our new understanding of biodiversity and ecosystems, however, suggests that we need to shift the emphasis away from simply cataloguing species richness to understanding what is called 'functional diversity'.

Merely cataloguing species is a gross, but relatively uninformative, measure of biodiversity, in the same way that body temperature is a gross measure of an individual's health, but doesn't tell us much about what is wrong when the temperature is too high. Such measures are important indicators, and can certainly serve as warnings when something is amiss. But they cannot be used by themselves to prescribe solutions. Just as doctors do not prescribe medicines solely on the basis of an anomalous body temperature, meaningful environmental policy measures cannot be based solely on dramatic declines in species richness.

Focusing on the functional diversity of an ecosystem . . . provides an important new approach to understanding . . . the relationship between biodiversity and ecosystem health.

This is where 'functional diversity' comes in. Functional diversity is a measure of how an individual species contributes to the workings of an ecosystem—for example, whether it enhances soil fertility by facilitating the fixation of nitrogen, whether it can tolerate drought or reduce soil erosion, or whether it is combustible and therefore more likely to increase the probability of fires. Functional diversity provides a better insight into the relationship between biodiversity and environmental processes than just the number of species in a given area.

Research in measuring functional diversity is still in its early stages. As a first step, scientists assume that the number of species in an ecosystem correlates with the overall functional diversity of that system. Current evidence supports this assumption—the more species you find in an area, the greater the functional diversity is likely to be. Conversely, if biodiversity declines dramatically, then functional diversity will almost certainly decline as well.

This suggests there will always be an important role for cataloguing species richness, which serves at least two purposes. First, it tells us when stop-gap measures need to be taken, as a dramatic decline in species richness suggests the need for strong species preservation, or for sustainable-use policies.

Secondly, species richness can serve as a proxy measure of functional diversity when functional diversity itself cannot be measured. In a typical rainforest, for example, there might be 300 species of trees per hectare and 3,400 species of beetles. And in a single gram of soil there could be around 4,000 strains of microbes. In practical terms, it is unlikely that scientists will be able to assess the contribution of each species to the overall functional diversity of the ecosystem, but just counting the number of species will give an approximate guide.

The consequences of biodiversity decline ... are complex, and our understanding of the reasons for such a decline ... is still in its early stages.

Nevertheless, focusing on the functional diversity of an ecosystem, and the contribution to it of each individual species, provides an important new approach to understanding the critical issue of the relationship between biodiversity and ecosystem health.

The Challenge to Policymakers

The consequences of biodiversity decline—whether occurring locally, regionally or globally—are complex, and our understanding of the reasons for such decline, where it is observed, is still in its early stages.

Governments, non-governmental organisations and academic institutions are currently investing a large amount of money and human resources in efforts to catalogue biodiversity. Strengthening taxonomy is certainly a critical step forward, similar to the way in which sequencing the human genome is the first step towards fully understanding the genetic basis of disease.

Ecosystem services—such as pollination, the production of clean water, and productive fisheries and forests— become less effective as biodiversity decreases.

But just as remedies for some diseases will come from understanding both the role of individual genes *and* the interactions among them, remedies for some environmental problems will require an understanding of both the functionality of individual species and of their interactions. In other words, understanding the relationship between biodiversity and ecosystems requires an understanding of the characteristic of species, their function within an ecosystem, and how they interact.

It is likely to be several decades before scientists can confidently say they have a good grasp of all these issues. But we already know enough to be able to predict that biodiversity-poor landscapes will recover more slowly from floods, droughts or fire; and that they will be less able than biodiversity-rich ones to resist invading species or the spread of emerging diseases.

We also know, on the basis of both observation and scientific research, that what are called ecosystem services—such as pollination, the production of clean water, and productive fisheries and forests—become less effective as biodiversity decreases. The challenge to policymakers is to design effective measures to prevent this from happening.

Dire Predictions of a Biodiversity Crisis May Be Overstated

Rhett A. Butler

Rhett A. Butler is an American wildlife advocate and founder of mongabay.com, an online magazine that seeks to raise interest in and appreciation of wild lands and wildlife, while examining the impact of emerging trends in climate, technology, economics, and finance on conservation and development

In recent years, scientists have warned of a looming biodiversity extinction crisis, one that will rival or exceed the five historic mass extinctions that occurred millions of years ago. Unlike these past extinctions, which were variously the result of catastrophic climate change, extraterrestrial collisions, atmospheric poisoning, and hyperactive volcanism, the current extinction event is one of our own making, fueled mainly by habitat destruction and, to a lesser extent, over-exploitation of certain species. While few scientists doubt species extinction is occurring, the degree to which it will occur in the future has long been [a] subject of debate in conservation literature. Looking solely at species loss resulting from tropical deforestation, some researchers have forecast extinction rates as high as 75 percent.

Now a new paper, published in *Biotropica*, argues that the most dire of these projections may be overstated. Using models that show lower rates of forest loss based on slowing population growth and other factors, Joseph Wright from the Smithsonian Tropical Research Institute in Panama and Helene Muller-Landau from the University of Minnesota say that species loss may be more moderate than the commonly cited fig-

Rhett A. Butler, "Just How Bad Is the Biodiversity Extinction Crisis? A Debate Erupts in the Halls of Conservation Science," *mongabay.com*, February 6, 2007. Reproduced by permission.

ures. While some scientists have criticized their work as "overly optimistic," prominent biologists say that their research has ignited an important discussion and raises fundamental questions about future conservation priorities and research efforts. This could ultimately result in more effective strategies for conserving biological diversity, they say.

"[Though] I believe [the Wright and Muller-Landau study] seriously understates the tropical biodiversity crisis," said William F. Laurance, an ecologist also from the Smithsonian Tropical Research Institute, their work "provides a clear rationale for projecting future species losses and highlights pressing research priorities" and "has precipitated a vigorous scientific debate." Laurance summarized and responded to Wright and Muller-Landau in a paper published in *TRENDS in Ecology and Evolution.*

Summary of Wright/Muller-Landau Conclusions

In their initial paper, titled "The Future of Tropical Forest Species" and published in 2006 in *Biotropica*, Wright and Muller-Landau demonstrate a relationship between human population density—especially in rural areas—and forest cover, suggesting that most deforestation results from subsistence slash-and-burn agriculture. Having established this relationship, the authors point to slowing rural population growth rates in most of the world resulting from lower birth rates and urbanization especially in Asia and Latin America.

Tropical forests have retreated to small areas before, namely during the Ice Ages.

On the basis of these lower rural growth rates, Wright and Muller-Landau argue that deforestation rates will slow. Overall, their model projects that net forest cover will not change much between now and 2030, though primary forest will be replaced by secondary forest. Using the species-area curve, which holds that there exists a tight correlation between the area of habitat and the number of species, the authors forecast a 21 percent to 24 percent extinction in Africa, 16 percent to 35 percent in Africa, and more moderate extinction rates in Latin America, though they don't offer an estimate. They argue that many species currently at risk from habitat loss will not go extinct in the end and instead will benefit from the projected abandonment of agricultural lands and subsequent regrowth of secondary forest in the absence of rural farmers practicing swidden agriculture.

The authors concede that while secondary forest is not as biodiverse as old growth or primary forest, in a historical context tropical forests have retreated to small areas before, namely during the Ice Ages under the refugia hypothesis. Further, they say, forest species that exist today have managed thus far to survive extensive hunting and land-clearing pressure from large sustained indigenous populations in the Amazon, Congo, and New Guinea.

While the argument seems straightforward, it is extremely controversial in the realm of conservation biology. Wright and Muller-Landau present their findings with several caveats which have helped spark a traditional scientific debate in which researchers respond deliberately, but sometimes heatedly, to one another through scientific journals.

Some Caveats

Wright and Muller-Landau caution that their extinction estimates are uncertain for several reasons. Their estimates of future forest losses may be wrong. The species-area curve [used in the study] may not work at small and large scales: specifically, deforestation in biodiversity hotspots—rich with endemic species—could throw off species-area calculations, or the species-area curve itself may not be applicable at global scale. Finally, and particularly contentious, the calculations do not account for differences in biological richness between primary and secondary forests.

In their papers, Wright and Muller-Landau acknowledge that extinction is likely to be higher in so-called biodiversity hotspots, areas with high numbers of endemic species that have already suffered large-scale habitat loss and are threatened by burgeoning population growth. Norman Myers, an Oxford University biologist who has figured prominently in conservation literature over the past 20 years, pioneered the concept of biodiversity hotspots when he identified 25 such hotspots covering 12 percent of Earth's land surface. He found that these were home to 44 percent of vascular plants and 35 percent of terrestrial vertebrates—a discovery that provided leverage for conservation initiatives. The 16 of these hotspots characterized by tropical forest have already lost an average of 90 percent of their forest cover, according to a 2002 *Conservation Biology* paper by Thomas Brooks and colleagues. Species-area math predicts that this depletion alone would result in the eventual extinction of 50 percent of the endemic species in these areas.

Wright and Muller-Landau argue that, while endemic hotspot species are at particular risk, "most tropical species are found outside these hotspots . . . and inhabit one of the four great blocks of tropical forest that once covered Indo-Malaya, Mesoamerica, the Amazon Basin and Guiana Shield, and the Congo Basin and humid western Africa. Here, for the groups that have been studied (largely plants, birds, and larger mammals), most species have large geographic distributions, which should buffer them from extinction."

Laurance disputes this claim, countering that "these areas also sustain numerous local endemics. . . . Even within seemingly monotonous expanses of forest, current and historical barriers, such as rivers, mountains and past forest refugia, have created complex patterns of species endemism. Hence, even the largest tropical forest tracts currently in existence contain many restricted endemics that are inherently vulnerable to habitat disruption."

The main point of contention over extinction is not whether it will occur but the degree of magnitude.

Wright and Muller-Landau also warn that "simple species-area considerations may not predict extinctions accurately at this scale" and that "species-area curves are crude tools," though to date, studies have found that speciesarea curves have thus far accurately predicted extinction. However, Laurance argues that Wright and Muller-Landau's treatment of remaining primary forest may well underestimate extinction because "they assume that surviving forests are merely shrinking in area, when in fact they are also being extensively fragmented." Laurance, who has spent more than 20 years studying the effects of fragmentation in the Amazon, knows that a fragmented forest is a less diverse one, since primary forest conditions can be so disrupted that it leads to the eventual disappearance of forest specialists. Further, Brooks and his colleagues point to extinction debt—the idea that species extinction, like global warming, has a time lag following forest clearing—a particular area where Wright and Muller-Landau may be understating extinction risk.

"The time lags observed between habitat loss and species extinction do not imply that a window of opportunity automatically opens for species recovery—this requires expensive, logistically challenging and unattainable conservation interventions for most species at risk," write Brooks and his colleagues. "The extinction momentum implied by the species-area relationship, termed the 'extinction debt' of past habitat loss is another critical hazard and inexorable threat that will drive future extinctions—even in a world with no net forest loss."

Old Growth Versus Secondary Growth Forest

While these are valid concerns, and ones that are acknowledged by Wright and Muller-Landau, the biggest questions arise from the biodiversity implications of their treatment of secondary forest versus primary forest.

They note that their model treats all forest cover, whether it is centuries-old rainforest or two-year-old secondary forest recovering from intensive logging and agricultural fires, as the same from a biodiversity standpoint. The problem, as any forest ecologist knows, is that secondary forest is less biodiverse than old growth forest. How much less biodiverse? That's the big question. No one knows. There is a lack of data that can shed definitive light on the issue. This so-called "data vacuum" is also a lightning rod for criticism of Wright and Muller-Landau.

The two authors say that the transition from primary forest to secondary forest will have minimal to moderate impact on global biodiversity. Their argument is based on the key assumption that most secondary forest will be allowed enough time (generally 20 to 40 years) to develop into forest that structurally resembles primary forest and can support species that typically require primary forest for survival. Their reasoning also assumes that sufficient areas of primary forest will persist to serve as refuges from which primary forest specialists can migrate to recovering and expanding secondary forests. Wright and Muller-Landau say that "secondary and degraded tropical forests are crucially important to conservation because of the vast areas of land involved," noting that "there are approximately 11,000,000 km² [square kilometers] of tropical forest today, of which 5,000,000 km are degraded or secondary forests."

While Toby Gardner, a scientist from the University of East Anglia who was lead author of a recent *Biotropica* article, agrees that secondary forests have conservation value, he argues that because they exist in such varying degrees of degradation, one can't presume that they will preserve most, or even some, biodiversity. "We challenge the validity of this assumption as secondary forests are highly heterogeneous, and their potential biodiversity value can be dramatically reduced," he says, due to factors including forest heavily degraded from fire, fragmentation, alien species, soil erosion and disrupted seed dispersal mechanisms. . . .

A Debate in a "Data Vacuum"

Wright and Muller-Landau's outlook, given the uncertainty of research, is of great concern to other scientists, who take a fundamentally different philosophical approach on how to proceed in a "data vacuum."

"The Wright and Muller-Landau study seems to violate the precautionary principle, which maintains that one should err on the side of caution in conservation matters," writes Laurance. "Concerns about potentially massive species losses have provided the political impetus for substantially expanding protected areas and conservation programs in the tropics. Even if future extinctions should be lower than many anticipate (partly because of these new conservation initiatives), the population sizes, geographical ranges and genetic variation of innumerable species are collapsing under the weight of burgeoning anthropogenic threats." "Hence, it seems too early to put an optimistic spin on the impending loss of tropical biodiversity; far better for our great-great grandchildren to make such a propitious finding, than to celebrate now and potentially leave our descendents to discover precisely the opposite." . . .

Common Ground

Harsh words aside, there are several important points of agreement between the contesting scientists. Brooks, Laurance, and Gardner seem to agree with Wright and Muller-Landau's conclusion that primary forest will continue to be depleted and converted to secondary forest at a rapid pace over the next 25 years, and that species extinction in the tropics will be significant—at minimum 10 percent at current rates. The main point of contention over extinction is not whether it will occur but the degree of magnitude—some projections are as high as 75 percent based on 90 percent loss of tropical forests, while the Wright and Muller-Landau estimates are considerably lower based on projections for less forest loss. All parties share common ground on the urgent need to further evaluate "the degree to which regenerating and degraded habitats can sustain tropical biodiversity" and, most importantly of all, to conserve old-growth tropical forests for the preservation of biodiversity.

Laurance highlights some of these points of agreement in his *TRENDS in Ecology and Evolution* paper.

"The Wright and Muller-Landau study provides a clear rationale for projecting future species losses and highlights pressing research priorities," writes Laurance. "Among these is the need to evaluate critically the degree to which regenerating and degraded habitats, which are increasing dramatically at the expense of old-growth forests, can sustain tropical biodiversity. Another priority is to advance our understanding of the proximate and ultimate drivers of forest loss, especially at regional and sub-regional scales, and how those drivers change in importance over time. Improving basic estimates of forest cover, loss, and regeneration for tropical nations is another key aim."

Continued research and urgent conservation action are needed to prevent species extinction.

Gardner agrees that more research is critical. He told *mongabay.com*: "Our main argument is that we simply do not know enough to say, and given this predicament a precautionary approach (focused on what we know is the most effective option for conserving biodiversity, the protection of mature native forest) is the most sensible way forward and the one least likely to encourage complacency." In principal, he agreed with one of Wright and Muller-Landau's recommendations, that old-growth species "will require new protected areas" and that more research will need to be conducted to assess the extinction risk faced by tropical forest species.

Wright and Muller-Landau add that there are several key questions that need to be addressed to improve the effectiveness of global conservation efforts. "First," they ask, "what proportion of tropical species is completely dependent on pristine, old-growth forests? Second," they continue, "how will global atmospheric and climatic changes affect old-growth and secondary tropical forests?" And further: "Where will today's conservation efforts be most effective? Should the focus be on countries in crisis today? . . . Should the focus be on countries likely to be in crisis in the future? . . . Or should the focus be on countries where there is even more breathing room?" They argue that "countries with large areas of extant forest, large projected human population growth rates, and limited protected area networks" should be the priority. Specifically, they point to the newly democratic country of Congo (DRC). "The Democratic Republic of the Congo is a prime example," they write. "Forest still covered 65 percent of its potential distribution in 2000, the human population is projected to increase by 312 percent by 2050, and just seven IUCN [World Conservation Union]—reserves include forest today (another 15 reserves include savannah or shrubland). The window of opportunity to establish protected areas will soon close in the Democratic Republic of the Congo and similar countries."

In the end, this is probably the most important conclusion of the ongoing debate: that continued research and urgent conservation action are needed to prevent species extinction.

Wright and Muller-Landau are up against a number of critics who say their claim that "the widely anticipated mass extinction of tropical forest species will be avoided" goes too far. But there is no doubt that even their "rosy outlook" shows a tropical extinction rate exceeding 10 percent, and that it also exempts the potential impact of human exploitation of certain species—albeit a relatively small universe of species. And there is also the proverbial 800-pound gorilla in the closet, climate change, which some fear could be responsible for mass extinction in its own right.

Biodiversity May Rise and Decline as Part of a Natural Earth Cycle

Space Daily

Space Daily *is a daily news source for space industry professionals.*

A detailed and extensive new analysis of the fossil records of marine animals over the past 542 million years has yielded a stunning surprise. Biodiversity appears to rise and fall in mysterious cycles of 62 million years for which science has no satisfactory explanation.

New Findings

The analysis, performed by researchers with the U.S. Department of Energy's Lawrence Berkeley National Laboratory (Berkeley Lab) and the University of California [UC] at Berkeley, has withstood thorough testing so that confidence in the results is above 99-percent.

"What we're seeing is a real and very strong signal that the history of life on our planet has been shaped by a 62 million year cycle, but nothing in present evolutionary theory accounts for it," said Richard Muller, a physicist who holds joint appointments with Berkeley Lab's Physics Division, and UC Berkeley's Physics Department. "While this signal has a huge presence in biodiversity, it can also be seen in both extinctions and originations."

Muller, and his grad student, Robert Rohde, presented their findings in the March 10, 2005 issue of the journal *Nature*.

In a commentary on this research in that same issue of *Nature*, UC Berkeley professor of earth and planetary sciences, James Kirchner, stated, "It is often said that the best discoveries in science are those that raise more questions than they answer, and that is certainly the case here."

Muller and Rohde discovered the 62 million year fossil diversity cycle after creating a computerized version of an exhaustive database compiled by the late University of Chicago paleontologist Jack Sepkoski. Entitled *Compendium of Fossil Marine Animal Genera,* Sepkoski's posthumously published database is the most complete reference available for the study of biodiversity and extinctions. It covers the Phanerozoic eon, the past half billion years during which multicellular organisms left abundant fossil records in rocks; uses genera, the level above species in taxonomy, because genera classifications are more manageable and less often revised than species classifications; and includes only marine fossils because the records are longer and better preserved than records of land fossils.

In general, longer-lived genera that are more diverse and widespread stand a better chance of resisting the 62 million year cycle.

For their study, Muller and Rohde defined fossil diversity as the number of distinct genera alive at any given time. This yielded a total of 36,380 genera, whose history the Berkeley scientists tracked over time, using the International Commission on Stratigraphy's 2004 time scale. "Putting the timescale in a chronologic format was critical to our findings, because there were no specific years assigned to the geologic timescale used by Sepkoski," Muller said. "We are the first to reconstruct diversity from the final version of Sepkoski's Compendium, and the first to use the 2004 geochronology time scale. In a sense, our work has verified the new time scale."

Muller and Rohde have been working on this study for nearly two years, and first discovered the 62 million year biodiversity cycle in November, 2003. They spent the next year trying to either knock it down or explain it.

No Clear Explanation

Despite examining 14 possible geophysical and astronomical causes of the cycles, no clear explanation emerged. Muller and Rohde each has his own favorite guess.

Muller suspects there is an astrophysical driving mechanism behind the 62 million year periodicity. "Comets could be perturbed from the Oort cloud by the periodic passage of the solar system through molecular clouds, Galactic arms, or some other structure with strong gravitational influence," Muller said. "But there is no evidence even suggesting that such a structure exists."

Rohde prefers a geophysical driver, possibly massive volcanic eruptions triggered by the rise of plumes to the earth's surface. Plumes are upwellings of hot material from near the earth's core that some scientists believe have the potential to reoccur on a periodic basis. "My hunch, far from proven," Rohde said, "is that every 62 million years the earth is releasing a burst of heat in the form of a plume formation event, and that when those plumes reach the surface they result in a major episode of flood volcanism. Such volcanism certainly has the potential to cause extinctions, but, right now there isn't enough geologic evidence to know whether flood basalts or plumes have been recurring at the right frequency."

In examining their results, Muller and Rohde found that the fossil diversity cycle is most evident when only short-lived genera (those that survived less than 45 million years) are considered. They also found that some organisms seem to be immune to the cycle, while others are exceptionally sensitive. For example, corals, sponges, arthropods and trilobites follow the cycle, but fish, squid and snails do not.

In general, longer-lived genera [organisms] that are more diverse and widespread stand a better chance of resisting the 62 million year cycle.

Muller and Rohde also found a second, less pronounced diversity cycle of 140 million years. "The 140 million year cycle is also strong, but we see only four oscillations in our 542 million year record," Muller said. "This means there is some chance that it could be accidental, rather than driven by some external mechanism." If it is real, the 140 million year fossil diversity cycle could be tied to a reported 140 million year cycle in Ice Ages. Said Rohde, "It is also possible that this 140 million year fossil diversity cycle is driven by passage through the arms of the Milky Way galaxy."

CHAPTER 2

What Plant and Animal Species Are Going Extinct?

Chapter Preface

Beginning in 2006 and continuing into the summer of 2007, an inexplicable phenomenon known as Colony Collapse Disorder (CCD) caused the deaths of billions of honeybees in twenty-seven states across the United States. For reasons scientists did not understand, adult bees abandoned the hives and disappeared, leaving the queen bee along with a population of young bees unable to take care of themselves. Without older bees to cover and protect them, the young bees cannot survive and the hive eventually collapses. Another odd part of the disorder is that the honey is usually left in the hive, but other bee colonies or predatory insects will not touch it, suggesting that something in the hive is repelling all insects.

According to the Apiary Inspectors of America, a group that tracks beekeeping in the United States, more than a quarter of the country's 2.4 million bee colonies had been lost as of 2007. Many beekeepers—people who make their living from bees—have reportedly lost 60 to 80 percent of their businesses. To keep their income flowing, some beekeepers began to transport their bees around the country in trucks, taking them to farms that need pollination services.

The American bee problem followed news of a widespread decline of bee diversity in other countries. A paper published in 2006 by the University of Leeds, for example, warned that many species of bees in Britain and the Netherlands have significantly declined or become extinct, along with the wild flowers and plants that they pollinate. Researchers found that many of the bee species studied only pollinate certain types of plants or that they required a specific habitat to survive. As these habitats declined, so did the bees. Conversely, the loss of bee diversity also causes a loss of plant diversity, because plants not pollinated by the bees are unable to reproduce.

Some experts say the bee losses also pose a serious threat to both the nation's and the world's agriculture industry because bees are essential for pollinating not only wild plants but also food crops, including many types of fruits, vegetables, and nuts. In fact, according to a 2006 study, about 35 percent of the world's crop production is dependent on pollinators such as bees, bats, and birds. In the United States, the U.S. Department of Agriculture estimates that 80 percent of all edible fruits and vegetables are pollinated by bees, and these crops, according to some estimates, are worth at least $14 billion annually. As Dr. Claire Kremen, an assistant professor at the University of California Berkeley's Department of Environmental Science, Policy, and Management, explained in an October 25, 2006, article published by *mongabay.com*, "You can thank a pollinator for one out of three bites of food you eat." Any significant biodiversity losses among these pollinators, therefore, could have a devastating impact on global food crops—an impact that could reduce world food production and result in significant economic losses.

As of 2008, no one was sure why the bees continued to disappear, although some experts speculate that a virus, a fungus, and a pesticide are the most likely suspects. Another possibility is that cell phone signals may be interfering with the bees' internal navigation abilities. Still other experts, however, suggest that the bee losses may be similar to past declines and that the problem may therefore be a cyclical one common in nature. Bee declines have been recorded as far back as 1896, for example, and each time, the colonies recovered and no cause was ever discovered.

Today's bee losses, however, may pose a bigger problem than similar declines in the past because they are taking place amid much broader biodiversity declines. Indeed, many scientists believe that human activities—such as urban sprawl that causes habitat losses and nonsustainable farming practices that rely on the heavy use of chemical pesticides and herbicides—are the fundamental cause of widespread biodiversity losses among bees as well as many other plant and animal species. The authors of the viewpoints in this chapter describe the extent of these species losses and the types of human activities that appear to be threatening plants and animals around the globe.

Without Action, Many Plant and Animal Species Will Be Extinct in Fifty Years

Philip Seaton

Philip Seaton taught biology for more than thirty years. He now works full time in orchid conservation. He is secretary to the Orchid Specialist Group of the IUCN/SSC, the World Conservation Union, and Orchid Conservation International, a registered charity.

The main reasons for [the biodiversity] ... crisis are well documented. The world's tropical forests are disappearing at an alarming rate, both due to logging for the timber trade (much of it illegal) and to land conversion to agriculture. Vast tracts of lowland forest have been converted to banana, oil palm or pineapple plantations. Large areas of the Amazon Basin are currently being converted to soya cultivation or pasture for cattle ranching. What is not always appreciated is that many of the world's temperate forests face a similar threat. Increased logging is taking place in the far east of Russia, for example, and clear felling is continuing along stretches of the northwestern coast of North America.

The potentially harmful effects of global warming are [also] of increasing concern. As average temperatures rise, habitats may change and become unsuitable for their resident plants and animals. To survive, many need to migrate to more suitable areas, but habitat fragmentation means that such species may literally have nowhere else to go.

The island of Mauritius [off the coast of Africa] is a tropical paradise. Most visitors do not realise that only around 1% of its original forest remains. The lush green forest canopy is

Philip Seaton, "Life in the Balance?" *Catalyst*, vol. 16, iss. 4, April 2006, pp. 1–3.
Copyright © 2006 Philip Allan Updates. Reproduced by permission.

largely made up of introduced exotic species—guava and privet. Invasion by exotic species is an increasing menace to natural populations. Of course, Mauritius was once home to the dodo, tragically extinct within less than 100 years of its discovery in 1598.

Sadly, [too,] examples of illegal and unsustainable hunting of animals for local trade and consumption, as well as for the international market, are easy to find. In China there is an illegal market in snow leopard skins and bones. The bones are used in traditional medicines, as are the gall bladders of bears. In parts of Africa where there is a shortage of protein, there is a thriving bush meat trade, including such wild animals as chimpanzees.

Why Should We Care?

There are various reasons why we should be concerned. The first is an economic argument. Illegal logging threatens the livelihoods of many local communities that depend on forest resources for employment and income. Trees bind the soil together and, particularly on steep slopes, prevent it being washed away by rainfall. Plants and animals are important sources of food, fibers and, potentially, undiscovered medicines.

After millions of years of evolution and coexistence, many people would argue that it is morally wrong to cause the extinction of plants and animals.

At the heart of the matter is the fact that we depend on other species for our continued existence on this planet. They are part of the fabric of life, and food chains and food webs may begin to unravel as key organisms are removed.

Ultimately, after millions of years of evolution and coexistence, many people would argue that it is morally wrong to cause the extinction of plants and animals.

What Is Being Done?

All of the above can make pretty depressing reading, but fortunately there appear to be an increasing number of people who care enough to be doing something, and more and more people are willing to pay to see wildlife in its natural habitat. The Central American country of Costa Rica, for example, derives more income from ecotourism than any other source. Here are just a few examples of the sorts of conservation activities and projects that are taking place around the world.

Mauritius kestrel: In situ conservation involves conservation of plants and animals in their natural habitats. The Mauritius kestrel declined to just four wild individuals, but captive breeding and subsequent reintroduction has saved this beautiful bird from extinction.

African elephants: One of the successes of the conservation community has been the international agreement banning trade in ivory and its products, thereby halting the lucrative market for poached tusks, and the catastrophic decline in African elephant populations.

Lady's slipper orchid: It is not only plants and animals in exotic places that are at risk. In Britain our native lady's slipper orchid declined to one individual plant remaining in a secret location somewhere in Yorkshire, after the plants had been dug up by collectors. Artificial pollinations were carried out by staff at the Royal Botanic Gardens, Kew [located in London, UK], the seeds germinated in the micropropagation unit, and a healthy population of seedlings was once again established in its natural habitat.

Sustainable Development

The key phrase in the vocabulary of today's conservationists is sustainable development. In Mexico many orchid species are used in religious festivals to decorate the altars. Not only are the flowers removed from the wild, but also sections of the plants, as this means that the flowers will remain fresh for a longer time. This leads to a decline in natural populations.

Projects are now being set up to store seed of these orchids for the future in germ banks, and laboratories are being established to raise orchids from seed for subsequent cultivation by the local people. The Millennium Seed Bank Project at Kew aims to conserve seeds representing 10% of the world's flora by 2010, concentrating particularly on semiarid areas, where most people live on land on which agriculture is marginal.

All Wild Fisheries May Be Extinct by 2050

Environment News Service

Environment News Service is a daily international wire service that presents late-breaking news about the environment.

All species of wild seafood that are currently fished are projected to collapse by the year 2050, according to a new four year study by an international team of ecologists and economists. Collapse is defined as 90 percent depletion.

Bad and Good News

The scientists warn that the loss of biodiversity is "profoundly" reducing the ocean's ability to produce seafood, resist diseases, filter pollutants, and rebound from stresses such as overfishing and climate change. "Whether we looked at tide pools or studies over the entire world's ocean, we saw the same picture emerging," says lead author Boris Worm of Dalhousie University. "In losing species we lose the productivity and stability of entire ecosystems. I was shocked and disturbed by how consistent these trends are—beyond anything we suspected."

The study published in the November 3 [2006] issue of the journal *Science* was based at the National Center of Ecological Analysis and Synthesis, NCEAS, funded by the National Science Foundation, the University of California and UC Santa Barbara. It contains some good news—the data show that ocean ecosystems still hold great ability to rebound. But the scientists found that every species lost causes a faster unraveling of the overall ecosystem. Conversely, every species recovered adds to overall productivity and stability of the ecosystem and its ability to withstand stresses. "Every species

Environment News Service, "Collapse of All Wild Fisheries Predicted in 45 Years," November 6, 2006. www.ens-newswire.com. Reproduced by permission.

matters," the scientists say. "Unless we fundamentally change the way we manage all the oceans species together, as working ecosystems, then this century is the last century of wild seafood," says co-author Steve Palumbi of Stanford University.

Recovery Still Possible

The analysis is the first to examine all existing data on ocean species and ecosystems, synthesizing historical, experimental, fisheries, and observational datasets to understand the importance of biodiversity at the global scale. The results reveal that progressive biodiversity loss not only impairs the ability of oceans to feed a growing human population, but also sabotages the stability of marine environments and their ability to recover from stresses.

"The data show us it's not too late," says Worm. "We can turn this around. But less than one percent of the global ocean is effectively protected right now. We won't see complete recovery in one year, but in many cases species come back more quickly than people anticipated—in three to five to 10 years. And where this has been done we see immediate economic benefits," Worm said.

The scientists on the NCEAS study say a pressing question for management is whether losses can be reversed. If species have not been pushed too far down, recovery can be fast—but there is also a point of no return as seen with species like northern Atlantic cod. In 1992, the cod population nearly reached a point of commercial extinction in waters off eastern Canada and Newfoundland, and a fishing moratorium was imposed. This moratorium has removed the main source of employment and income for thousands of fishermen from hundreds of small fishing communities. "This isn't predicted to happen, this is happening now," says co-author Nicola Beaumont an ecological economist with the Plymouth Marine Laboratory. "If biodiversity continues to decline, the marine environment will not be able to sustain our way of life, indeed it may not be able to sustain our lives at all."

Collapses are hastened by the decline in overall health of the ecosystem. Fish rely on the clean water, prey populations and diverse habitats that are linked to higher diversity systems. The study suggests that these relationships point to the need for managers to consider all species together rather than continuing with single species management. "This analysis provides the best documentation I have ever seen regarding biodiversity's value," adds Peter Kareiva, a former Brown University professor and U.S. government fisheries manager who now leads science efforts at The Nature Conservancy. "There is no way the world will protect biodiversity without this type of compelling data demonstrating the economic value of biodiversity," Kareiva said.

Other Benefits of a Healthy Ocean

Impacts of species loss go beyond declines in seafood. Human health risks emerge as depleted coastal ecosystems become vulnerable to invasive species, disease outbreaks and noxious algal blooms.

Many of the economic activities along our coasts rely on diverse systems and the healthy waters they supply. "The ocean is a great recycler," explains Palumbi, "It takes sewage and recycles it into nutrients, it scrubs toxins out of the water, and it produces food and turns carbon dioxide into food and oxygen."

Restoring marine biodiversity through an ecosystem based management approach ... is essential to avoid serious threats to global food security.

But in order to provide these services, the ocean needs all its working parts, the millions of plant and animal species that inhabit the sea.

Criticism of the Study

The study drew immediate criticism from the Australian government, which "categorically rejects" claims made by northern hemisphere scientists led by Canada's Dalhousie University that Australia's fisheries are set to collapse. "The reality is Australia is a world leader in fisheries and oceans management," Australian Fisheries Minister Senator Eric Abetz said Friday [November 4, 2006]. "While we obviously welcome any serious scientific contribution, instead of trying to tar us all with the same brush, these scientists should instead be singling Australia out as an example to the world of how to ensure fisheries sustainability," said Abetz. "Frankly, we get a bit annoyed at northern hemisphere scientists, whose fisheries management often leaves a lot to be desired, making sensationalist predictions about the state of Australian fisheries from half a world away," he said.

Australia has a comprehensive plan to ensure the sustainability of Commonwealth fish stocks for generations to come, said Abetz, emphasizing that of the world's area of marine protected areas, some one third is in Australian waters.

Restoring Biodiversity Is Essential

The strength of the NCEAS study is the consistent agreement of theory, experiments and observations across widely different scales and ecosystems, the participating scientists say. The study analyzed 32 controlled experiments, observational studies from 48 marine protected areas, and global catch data from the UN's Food and Agriculture Organization's database of all fish and invertebrates worldwide from 1950 to 2003. The scientists also looked at a 1,000 year time series for 12 coastal regions, drawing on data from archives, fishery records, sediment cores and archeological data.

"We see an accelerating decline in coastal species over the last 1,000 years, resulting in the loss of biological filter capacity, nursery habitats, and healthy fisheries," says co-author

Heike Lotze of Dalhousie University who led the historical analysis of Chesapeake Bay, San Francisco Bay, the Bay of Fundy, and the North Sea, among other bodies of water.

Examination of protected areas worldwide show[s] that restoration of biodiversity increased productivity four-fold in terms of catch per unit effort and made ecosystems 21 percent less susceptible to environmental and human caused fluctuations on average. The buffering impact of species diversity also generates long term insurance values that must be incorporated into future economic valuation and management decisions. "Although there are short-term economic costs associated with preservation of marine biodiversity, over the long term biodiversity conservation and economic development are complementary goals," says co-author Ed Barbier, an economist from the University of Wyoming.

The authors conclude that restoring marine biodiversity through an ecosystem based management approach—integrated fisheries management, pollution control, maintenance of essential habitats and creation of marine reserves—is essential to avoid serious threats to global food security, coastal water quality and ecosystem stability.

200-Year-Old Tropical Rainforests Are Disappearing at a Rate Never Seen Before

Geographical

Geographical is the official magazine of the Royal Geographical Society, a professional organization based in London that works to advance geographical science.

The tropical forests originated almost 200 million years ago during the early days of the dinosaurs. They ware huddled together in the giant supercontinent Pangaea, which was centred around the equator and covered by huge ferns and early forms of conifer trees.

At the same time as the modern forest was evolving, Pangaea was gradually breaking up. First Australia and Antarctica (which itself was once forested) broke away. Then the Americas began to move off. Later, Madagascar separated from Africa. At each stage, evolution started to take a different course. Thus the forest monkeys that evolved in the Old and New Worlds, while coming from the same ancient stock and living similar lives in similar environments, are anatomically quite distinct. Similarly, lemurs [a small, nocturnal primate] survived only in Madagascar, in part because the island had no large predators.

Since the days of Pangaea, the planet's climate has cooled somewhat. But throughout the wet tropics, where it typically rains most of the year, rainforests remain the natural vegetation. They are the planet's largest reservoir of biological diversity, containing more than half of its plant and animal species. They also play a vital role in maintaining ecological services such as the water and carbon cycles, by storing carbon, conserving soils and generating rainfall.

Rainforest Regions

The largest of these forests is in the Amazon Basin. The basin contains roughly two thirds of the world's surviving tropical rainforests, representing some 30 per cent of all the biological material on the land surface of the planet. The forest receives so much rain that the river running through it has five times the flow of the river with the next largest flow, the Congo, which itself runs through the world's second largest continuous tract of rainforest, in Central Africa.

The scale and pace of . . . deforestation over the past 200 years dwarfs anything seen before.

The third great rainforest region straddles Southeast Asia from Myanmar through Malaysia and Indonesia and on to the islands of the South Pacific, including New Guinea and the Solomons. Smaller patches also survive in West Africa, Central America, northern Australia, the Indian subcontinent and on some tropical islands, but most of the forests in these areas have been cleared for farming.

The vast majority of rainforests are found in the basins of great rivers. Most are on dry land—creating dark and surprisingly vegetation-free "cathedrals", as [biologist] Edward Wilson calls them, beneath the canopy, where "there is almost never a need to slash a path with a machete through tangled vegetation". But some occupy land that is seasonally inundated by the rivers, as in the Amazon upstream of Manaus, or sit on top of great peat swamps, as in Borneo and Sumatra.

Other rainforests form on coasts, as dense mangrove thickets. The biggest of these are the forests of the Sunderbans on the Ganges delta of India and Bangladesh—the famed domain of the Bengal tiger—and on New Guinea, the world's largest tropical island.

And finally there are distinctive cloud forests in the near-permanent clouds of tropical uplands such as the eastern slopes of the Andes, the highlands of Central Africa, parts of Central America and the remote interior of New Guinea. The trunks of the trees here are short and gnarled by comparison with the tall straight trees of the lowlands. But their canopies are among the richest of all, with immense growths of ferns, orchids, lichens and mosses luxuriating in the damp of the clouds.

There are probably very few truly virgin forests left on Earth. Most have been burned, replanted or otherwise influenced by humans at some time or another. Ecologists now see them less as ancient, unchanging, pristine habitats and more as examples of nature's dynamism and instability.

It's only recently that humankind has come to appreciate the wider value of rainforests, in conserving biological diversity.

Deforestation Threats

Pristine or not, the scale and pace of anthropogenic deforestation over the past 200 years dwarfs anything seen before. Tropical forests once covered 25 million square kilometres, 16 per cent of the Earth's land surface. Today, this figure is less than ten million square kilometres. Half of the former forests are now permanent farms, another quarter are pastures and the final quarter is under some form of shifting cultivation.

The deforestation of the Brazilian Amazon has spread from east to west as roads and development projects have penetrated the forest. Much of Indonesia's forest has been converted into farms as a result of the national transmigration program, which has moved some four million people from densely populated areas to forested provinces such as Kalimantan and West Papua (formerly Irian Jaya).

Piecemeal forest removal has also fragmented forest regions, which has a disproportionate effect on species diversity by limiting the ecosystem's ability to recover from catastrophes such as fires and by reducing gene flow between populations.

It's only recently that humankind has come to appreciate the wider value of rainforests, in conserving biological diversity and providing ecological services. Historically, however, rainforests were the playgrounds of explorers, biologists, pharmacists and entrepreneurs, all eager to make their mark or their fortune.

The Other Tropical Forests

Rainforests aren't the only ecologically and economically important forests found in the tropics. Located in the shallow tidal waters of estuaries and other coastal areas are vast stands of salt-tolerant trees and shrubs known as mangroves. These forests require slow currents, no frost and plenty of fine sediment in which the plants can set their roots. Their muddy waters, rich in nutrients from decaying leaves and wood, are home to a wide variety of organisms, from sponges, worms and crustaceans to marine mammals, birds, snakes and crocodiles.

Mangroves protect coastlines by absorbing the force of storms, act as fish nurseries and help feed life farther out to sea. Queensland's mangroves, for instance, do much to sustain the Great Barrier Reef, the world's largest coral-reef system. Mangroves are also strongly linked to the presence of shoals of shrimp further offshore.

The seedlings of members of the main tree genus, Rhizophora, cure a sore mouth and Filipinos use foliage from Nypa trees to thatch roofs and the trees' sap to make alcohol.

Mangroves are, nonetheless, under grave threat. Their communal benefits are no match for the quick profits that can be made from chopping them down for timber, draining them for farming and urban development or converting them into salt pans and shrimp ponds.

Acid Oceans May Kill Off the World's Coral Reefs

Juliet Eilperin

Juliet Eilperin is a staff writer for the Washington Post, *a Washington, D.C.-based daily newspaper.*

The escalating level of carbon dioxide in the atmosphere is making the world's oceans more acidic, government and independent scientists say. They warn that, by the end of the century, the trend could decimate coral reefs and creatures that underpin the sea's food web.

By taking up one-third of the atmosphere's carbon dioxide ... oceans are transforming their pH level.

Ocean Acidification

Although scientists and some politicians have just begun to focus on the question of ocean acidification, they describe it as one of the most pressing environmental threats facing Earth. "It's just been an absolute time bomb that's gone off both in the scientific community and, ultimately, in our public policymaking," said Rep. Jay Inslee (D-Wash.), who received a two-hour briefing on the subject in May with five other House members. "It's another example of when you put gigatons of carbon dioxide into the atmosphere, you have these results none of us would have predicted."

Thomas E. Lovejoy, president of the H. John Heinz III Center for Science, Economics and the Environment, has just rewritten the paperback edition of *Climate Change and Biodiversity*, his latest book, to highlight the threat of ocean acidification. "It's the single most profound environmental change I've learned about in my entire career," he said last week [last week of June 2006].

A coalition of federal and university scientists is to issue a report today [July 5, 2006], describing how carbon dioxide emissions are, in the words of a press release from the National Center for Atmospheric Research and the National Oceanic and Atmospheric Administration, "dramatically altering ocean chemistry and threatening corals and other marine organisms that secrete skeletal structures."

For decades, scientists have viewed the oceans' absorption of carbon dioxide as an environmental plus, because it mitigates the effects of global warming. But by taking up one-third of the atmosphere's carbon dioxide—much of which stems from exhaust from automobiles, power plants and other industrial sources—oceans are transforming their pH level.

The pH level, measured in "units," is a calculation of the balance of a liquid's acidity and its alkalinity. The lower a liquid's pH number, the higher its acidity; the higher the number, the more alkaline it is. The ph level for the world's oceans was stable between 1000 and 1800, but has dropped one-tenth of a unit since the Industrial Revolution, according to Christopher Langdon, a University of Miami marine biology professor.

Scientists expect ocean pH levels to drop by another 0.3 units by 2100, which could seriously damage marine creatures that need calcium carbonate to build their shells and skeletons. Once absorbed in seawater, carbon dioxide forms carbonic acid and lowers ocean pH, making it harder for corals, plankton and tiny marine snails (called pteropods) to form their body parts.

Ken Caldeira, a chemical oceanographer at Stanford University who briefed lawmakers along with NCAR marine ecologist Joan Kleypas, said oceans are more acidic than they have has been for "many millions of years." "What we're doing in the next decade will affect our oceans for millions of years," Caldeira said. "CO_2 levels are going up extremely rapidly, and it's overwhelming our marine systems."

An Undeniable Phenomenon

Some have questioned global-warming predictions based on computer models, but ocean acidification is less controversial because it involves basic chemistry. "You can duplicate this phenomenon by blowing into a straw in a glass of water and changing the water's pH level," Lovejoy said. "It's basically undeniable."

Hugo A. Loáiciga, a geography professor at the University of California at Santa Barbara, is one of the few academics to question the phenomenon. A groundwater hydrologist, Loáiciga published a paper in the May edition of the American Geophysical Union's journal that suggested the oceans may not become so acidic, because enough carbonate material will help restore equilibrium to them.

Loáiciga wrote that although seawater in certain regions may become more acidic over time, "on a global scale and over the time scales considered (hundreds of years), there would not be accentuated changes in either seawater salinity or acidity from the rising concentration of atmospheric CO_2."

Coupled with the higher sea temperatures that climate change produces . . . corals may not survive by the end of the century.

Two dozen scientists have written a response questioning this assumption, since it would take thousands of years for such material to reach the oceans from land. "The paper by Loáiciga ignores decades of scholarship, presents inappropriate calculations and draws erroneous conclusions that simply do not apply to real ocean," they wrote. They added that, unless carbon dioxide levels in the atmosphere stabilize soon, the seas will soon exceed the Environmental Protection Agency's recommended acidity limits.

Scientists have conducted a few ocean acidification experiments in recent years. All have shown that adding carbon dioxide to the water slows corals' growth rate and can dissolve pteropods' [a type of mollusk] shells.

Langdon, who conducted an experiment between 1996 and 2003 in Columbia University's Biosphere 2 lab in Tucson, concluded that corals grew half as fast in aquariums when exposed to the level of carbon dioxide projected to exist by 2050. Coupled with the higher sea temperatures that climate change produces, Langdon said, corals may not survive by the end of the century. "It's going to be on a global scale and it's also chronic," Langdon said of ocean acidification. "Twenty-four/seven, it's going to be stressing these organisms. . . . These organisms probably don't have the adaptive ability to respond to this new onslaught."

Stanford University marine biologist Robert B. Dunbar has studied the effect of increased carbon dioxide on coral reefs in Israel and Australia's Great Barrier Reef. "What we found in Israel was the community is dissolving," Dunbar said.

Caldeira has mapped out where corals exist today and the pH levels of the water in which they thrive; by the end of the century, no seawater will be as alkaline as where they live now. If carbon dioxide emissions continue at their current levels, he said, "It's say 'goodbye' to coral reefs."

The Effect on Other Marine Species

Although the fate of plankton and marine snails may not seem as compelling as vibrantly colored coral reefs, they are critical to sustaining marine species such as salmon, redfish, mackerel and baleen whales. "These are groups everyone depends on, and if their numbers go down there are going to be reverberations throughout the food chain," said John Guinotte, a marine biologist at the Marine Conservation Biology Institute. "When I see marine snails' shells dissolving while they're alive, that's spooky to me."

Rep. Rush D. Holt (D-N.J.), a scientist by training, attended the congressional briefing on ocean acidification. He said these developments are "new to me, which was surprising because I usually keep up with things."

"The changes in our climate are severe and urgent even if it weren't for this, but this just adds impact and urgency to the situation," Holt said.

America's Wild Bird Populations Are Declining

National Audubon Society

The National Audubon Society is an organization of community-based chapters that conserve and restore natural ecosystems, focusing on birds, other wildlife, and their habitats for the benefit of humanity and the Earth's biological diversity.

A new analysis by the National Audubon Society reveals that populations of some of America's most familiar and beloved birds have taken a nosedive over the past forty years, with some down as much as 80 percent. The dramatic declines are attributed to the loss of grasslands, healthy forests and wetlands, and other critical habitats from multiple environmental threats such as sprawl, energy development, and the spread of industrialized agriculture. The study notes that these threats are now compounded by new and broader problems including the escalating effects of global warming. In concert, they paint a challenging picture for the future of many common species and send a serious warning about our increasing toll on *local* habitats and the environment itself.

"These are not rare or exotic birds we're talking about—these are the birds that visit our feeders and congregate at nearby lakes and seashores and yet they are disappearing day by day," said Audubon Chairperson and former EPA [Environmental Protection Agency] Administrator, Carol Browner. "Their decline tells us we have serious work to do, from protecting local habitats to addressing the huge threats from global warming."

National Audubon Society, "Disappearing Common Birds Send Environmental Wake-Up Call," www.audubon.org, June 14, 2007. Reproduced by permission.

Threatened Species

Species on Audubon's list of 20 *Common Birds in Decline* have seen their populations plummet at least 54 percent since 1967. The following are among those hardest hit:

- *Northern Bobwhite* populations are down 82 percent and have largely vanished from northern parts of their range in Wisconsin, Michigan, New York and New England mainly due to loss of suitable habitat to development, agricultural expansion and plantation-style forestry practices.

- *Evening Grosbeaks* that range from mountains of the west to northern portions of the east coast show population declines of nearly 78 percent amid increasing habitat damage and loss from logging, mining, drilling and development.

- *Northern Pintail* populations in the continental U.S. are down nearly 78 percent due to expanding agricultural activity in their prairie pothole breeding grounds.

- *Greater Scaup* populations that breed in Alaska, but winter in the Great Lakes and along Atlantic to Pacific Coasts are being hard hit by global warming induced melting of permafrost and invasion of formerly-southern species; populations are down approximately 75 percent.

- *Eastern Meadowlarks*, down 71 percent, are declining as grasslands are lost to industrialized agricultural practices. Increased demand for biofuel crops threatens increased agricultural use of lands that are currently protected, making both Eastern and Western Meadowlarks even more vulnerable.

- *Common Terns*, which nest on islands and forage for fish near ocean coasts, lakes and rivers, are vulnerable to development, pollution and sea level rise from global warming. Populations in unmanaged colonies have dropped as much as 70 percent, making the species' outlook increasingly dependent on targeted conservation efforts.

- *Snow Buntings*, which breed in Alaska and northern Canada, are suffering from the loss of fragile tundra habitat as global warming alters and disrupts the Arctic's delicate ecological balance; populations are down 64 percent.

- *Rufous Hummingbird* populations have declined 58 percent as a result of the loss or forest habitat to logging and development, in both their breeding range in the Pacific Northwest and their wintering sites in Mexico.

- *Whip-poor-wills*, down 57 percent, are vulnerable to fragmentation and alteration of their forest habitat from development and poor forest management practices.

- *Little Blue Herons* now number 150,000 in the U.S. and 110,000 in Mexico, down 54 percent in the U.S. Their decline is driven by wetland loss from development and degradation of water quality, which limits their food supply.

Public response will shape the long-term outlook for the listed species.

Habitat Losses

Overall, agricultural and development pressures have driven grassland birds to some of the worst declines, followed closely by shrub, wetland and forest-dependent species. "Direct habitat loss continues to be a leading cause for concern," said Audubon Bird Conservation Director and analysis author, Greg

Butcher, PhD. "But now we're seeing the added impact of large-scale environmental problems and policies."

Butcher notes that global warming is damaging some key habitats and speeding the spread of invasive species that spur further declines. Mounting demand for corn-based fuels is expected to result in increased use of marginal farmland that currently serves as important habitat. The fate of species such as Eastern Meadowlarks and Loggerhead Shrikes could hinge on efforts to conserve these areas. "People who care about the birds and about human quality of life need to get involved in habitat protection at home, in pushing for better state and national protections and in making changes in their daily routines," Butcher adds.

The Long-Term Outlook

Public response will shape the long-term outlook for the listed species. Unlike WatchList birds, these *Common Birds in Decline* are not in immediate danger of extinction, despite global populations as low as 500,000 for some species—the threshold for a "common bird" designation. But even birds with significantly higher overall populations are experiencing sharp declines, and with their populations down sharply, their ecological roles are going unfilled and their ultimate fate is uncertain. Audubon leaders hope the multiple threats to the birds people know will prompt individuals to take multiple actions, both locally and directed toward state and national policies.

Audubon's *Common Birds in Decline* list stems from the first-ever analysis combining annual sighting data from Audubon's century-old Christmas Bird Count program with results of the annual Breeding Bird Survey conducted by the U.S. Geological Survey. "This is a powerful example of how tens of thousands of volunteer birders, pooling their observations, can make an enormous difference for the creatures they care the most about," said noted natural history writer Scott Weidensaul. "Thanks to their efforts, we have the information.

Now all of us—from birders to policy makers—need to take action to keep these species from declining even further."

"Fortunately, people's actions can still make a difference," Audubon's Greg Butcher adds. "Average citizens can change the fate of these birds just as average citizens helped us confirm the trouble they face."

The Risk of Species Extinction Is Increasing Due to Global Warming

John Roach

John Roach is a reporter for National Geographic News, *a Web site produced by the National Geographic Society, a nonprofit, educational, and scientific organization.*

By 2050, rising temperatures exacerbated by human-induced belches of carbon dioxide and other greenhouse gases could send more than a million of Earth's land-dwelling plants and animals down the road to extinction, according to a recent study.

A Global Study

"Climate change now represents at least as great a threat to the number of species surviving on Earth as habitat-destruction and modification," said Chris Thomas, a conservation biologist at the University of Leeds in the United Kingdom. Thomas is the lead author of the study published . . . [in 2004] in the science journal *Nature*. His co-authors included 18 scientists from around the world, making this the largest collaboration of its type.

Townsend Peterson, an evolutionary biologist at the University of Kansas in Lawrence and one of the study's co-authors, said the paper allows scientists for the first time to "get a grip" on the impact of climate change as far as natural systems are concerned. "A lot of us are in this to start to get a handle on what we are talking about," he said. "When we talk about the difference between half a percent and one percent of carbon dioxide emissions what does that mean?"

The researchers worked independently in six biodiversity-rich regions around the world, from Australia to South Africa, plugging field data on species distribution and regional climate into computer models that simulated the ways species' ranges are expected to move in response to temperature and climate changes. "We later met and decided to pool results to produce a more globally relevant look at the issue," said Lee Hannah, a climate change biologist with Conservation International's Center for Applied Biodiversity Science in Washington, D.C.

The predicted range of climate change by 2050 will place 15 to 35 percent of the 1,103 species studies at risk of extinction.

Study Results

According to the researchers' collective results, the predicted range of climate change by 2050 will place 15 to 35 percent of the 1,103 species studied at risk of extinction. The numbers are expected to hold up when extrapolated globally, potentially dooming more than a million species. "These are first-pass estimates, but they put the problem in the right ballpark ... I expect more detailed studies to refine these numbers and to add data for additional regions, but not to change the general import of these findings," said Hannah.

Writing in an accompanying commentary to the study in *Nature*, J. Alan Pounds of the Monteverde Cloud Forest Reserve in Costa Rica, and Robert Puschendorf, a biologist at the University of Costa Rica, say these estimates "might be optimistic." As global warming interacts with other factors such as habitat-destruction, invasive species, and the buildup of carbon dioxide in the landscape, the risk of extinction increases even further, they say.

In agreement with the study authors, Pounds and Puschendorf say taking immediate steps to reduce greenhouse gas emissions is imperative to constrain global warming to the minimum predicted levels and thus prevent many of the extinctions from occurring. "The threat to life on Earth is not just a problem for the future. It is part of the here and now," they write.

Climate Scenarios

The researchers based their study on minimum, mid-range, and maximum future climate scenarios based on information released by the United Nations' Intergovernmental Panel on Climate Change (IPCC) in 2001. According to the IPCC, temperatures are expected to rise from somewhere between 1.5 and more than 4 degrees Fahrenheit (0.8 and more than 2 degrees Celsius) by the year 2050. "Few climate scientists around the world think that 2050 temperatures will fall outside those bounds," said Thomas. "In some respects, we have been conservative because almost all future climate projections expect more warming and hence more extinction between 2050 and 2100."

Rapid reductions of greenhouse gas emissions may allow some of these species to hang on.

In addition, the researchers accounted for the ability of species to disperse or successfully move to a new area, thus preventing climate change-induced extinction. They used two alternatives: one where species couldn't move at all, the other assuming unlimited abilities for movement. "We are trying to bracket the truth," said Peterson. "If you bracket the truth and look at the two endpoints and they give the same general message, then you can start to believe it."

Outside of the small group of researchers working directly on the impacts of climate change to species diversity, "the numbers will come as a huge shock," said Thomas.

Extinction Prevention

The researchers point out that there is a significant gap between the low and high ends of the species predicted to be on the road to extinction by 2050. Taking action to ensure the climate ends up on the low end of the range is vital to prevent catastrophic extinctions. "We need to start thinking about the fullest of costs involved with our activities, the real costs of what we do in modern society," said Peterson.

Thomas said that since there may be a large time lag between the climate changing and the last individual of a doomed species dying off, rapid reductions of greenhouse gas emissions may allow some of these species to hang on. "The only conservation action that really makes sense, at a global scale, is for the international community to minimize warming through reduced emissions and the potential establishment of carbon-sequestration programs," he said.

CHAPTER 3

Are Food Production Activities Harming the Earth's Biodiversity?

Chapter Preface

Advocates of organic farming—that is, farming without the use of synthetic chemical pesticides, herbicides, and fertilizers—have long claimed that this more natural method of agriculture boosts animal and plant biodiversity. The absence of poisonous chemicals, supporters argue, makes organic farms less dangerous for all wildlife, including larger mammals such as rabbits and squirrels as well as smaller creatures such as birds and insects. Also, in many cases, organic fields are bounded by rows of shrubs, grasses, trees, and other natural areas that provide berries and seeds—foods that are attractive to a variety of insects, birds, and bats. In addition, organic farms typically grow a wider variety of crops than conventional farms, and they often have livestock—both features that provide a richer habitat for area wildlife.

Recent studies have helped support the link between biodiversity and organic farming. For example, a five-year study of 180 farms in Britain, sponsored by the British government and reported in 2005, found that organic farms contained 85 percent more plant species, 33 percent more bats, 17 percent more spiders, and 5 percent more birds than conventional farms. Scientists involved in the study attributed the greater biodiversity to the exclusion of synthetic pesticides and fertilizers from the organic farms, and they urged that more organic farming could help restore biodiversity within agricultural landscapes throughout the country.

Organic farming practices are not only beneficial for larger wildlife, however. Other studies have found greater soil fertility and more biodiversity in beneficial soil organisms at organic farms. A report published in 2004, by researchers from two British government agencies, for example, reviewed data from 76 studies of farms in Europe, Canada, New Zealand, and the United States. The report concluded that organic farming techniques help to promote biodiversity throughout the food chain—all the way from birds and bats down to tiny bacteria and earthworms in the soil. In fact, researchers said that even farms that adopt just a few organic practices, such as eliminating chemical weed-killing methods for mechanical ones, can create significant increases in biodiversity.

An earlier study published in 2002 in the journal *Science* reached similar conclusions. In the study, the Research Institute for Organic Agriculture, an organic agriculture research group based in Switzerland and Germany, looked at both organic and conventional farming systems over a 21-year period. Researchers found that soil fertility on organic farms was much higher than on conventional farms; in fact, more than twice as many soil microorganisms, earthworms, and ground beetles were found in the organic plots. This rich soil biodiversity, the study said, was the secret to high crop yields on organic farms, despite their low use of fertilizers and pesticides. Indeed, the study concluded that, overall, organic farms produced only about 20 percent less food than conventional farming methods, without causing damage to the soil or the environment.

The point about agricultural yield is an important one because critics of organic agriculture often assert that the lower yields from organic farming is the reason it is not feasible as a way to feed the world's growing population. Critics of organic farming argue that because of the method's lower yields, organic farms require much more land to produce the same amount of food now produced by conventional, or industrial, farming methods. As the world population surges in coming decades to an expected 9 billion by 2050, these critics say that there will not be enough land to support organic agriculture and that only large-scale industrial farms will be able to keep up with the demands for food.

Advocates of organic farming counter that any loss in yields is more than made up for by the ecological and biodiversity benefits of organic farming. The practices of conventional agriculture, they say, are causing severe environmental damage, including loss of topsoil, decrease in soil fertility, surface and ground water contamination, and loss of genetic diversity. Many experts believe such practices are not sustainable over the long run and that organic methods must be adopted on a widespread scale to keep the environment healthy, preserve biodiversity, and ensure that food production can be continued indefinitely.

This debate about how food should be produced is expanded upon by the authors of the following viewpoints. Topics discussed in this chapter touch upon the debate concerning organic and conventional farming; the risks and benefits of biotechnology; and the challenges in preserving marine food sources.

Industrial Agriculture Is One of the Main Threats to Biodiversity

Miguel A. Altieri

Miguel A. Altieri, Ph.D., teaches agroecology in the Department of Environmental Science, Policy and Management at University of California at Berkeley. He is also the General Coordinator for the United Nations Development Programme's Sustainable Agriculture Networking and Extension Programme and the author of numerous books and articles.

Agriculture implies the simplification of nature's biodiversity and reaches an extreme form in crop monoculture. The end result is the production of an artificial ecosystem requiring constant human intervention. In most cases, this intervention is in the form of agrochemical inputs which, in addition to boosting yields, result in a number of undesirable environmental and social costs.

Agriculture's Threat to Biodiversity

Global threats to biodiversity should not be foreign to agriculturalists, since agriculture, which covers about 25–30% of the world land area, is perhaps one of the main activities affecting biological diversity. It is estimated that the global extent of cropland increased from around 265 million hectares in 1700 to around 1.5 billion hectares today, predominantly at the expense of forest habitats. Very limited areas remain totally unaffected by agriculture-induced land use changes.

Clearly, agriculture implies the simplification of the structure of the environment over vast areas, replacing nature's di-

Miguel A. Altieri, "Fatal Harvest: Old and New Dimensions of the Ecological Tragedy of Modern Agriculture," *Journal of Business Administration and Policy Analysis*, vol. 30-31, 2002, p. 239. Copyright © 2002 *Journal of Business Administration and Policy Analysis*. Reproduced by permission.

versity with a small number of cultivated plants and domesticated animals. In fact, the world's agricultural landscapes are planted with only some 12 species of grain crops, 23 vegetable crop species, and about 35 fruit and nut crop species; that is no more than 70 plant species spread over approximately 1,440 million [hectares] of presently cultivated land in the world. This is in sharp contrast with the diversity of plant species found within one hectare of a tropical rainforest which typically contains over 100 species of trees. Of the 7,000 crop species used in agriculture, only 120 are important at a national level. An estimated 90% of the world's calorie intake comes from just 30 crops, a small sample of the vast crop diversity available (Jackson and Jackson 2002).

As the industrial [agriculture] model was introduced into the developing world, agricultural diversity has been eroded.

The process of biodiversity simplification associated with industrial agriculture can affect biodiversity in various ways:

- Expansion of agricultural land with loss of natural habitats

- Conversion into homogenous agricultural landscapes with low habitat value for wildlife

- Loss of wild species and beneficial agrobiodiversity as a direct consequence of agrochemical inputs and other practices

- Erosion of valuable genetic resources through increased use of uniform high-yielding varieties

As the industrial model was introduced into the developing world, agricultural diversity has been eroded as monoculture has started to dominate. For example, in Bangladesh the promotion of Green Revolution rice led to a loss of diversity including nearly 7,000 traditional rice varieties and many fish species. Similarly in the Philippines, the introduction of HYV [high yield variety] rice displaced more than 300 traditional rice varieties. In the North similar losses in crop diversity [are] occurring. Eighty-six percent of the 7,000 apple varieties used in the U.S. between 1804 and 1904 are no longer in cultivation; of 2,683 pear varieties, 88% are no longer available. In Europe thousands of varieties of flax and wheat vanished following the take-over by modern variants.

Today, monoculture [agriculture] has increased dramatically worldwide.

Genetic Homogenization and Ecological Vulnerability

Modern agriculture is shockingly dependent on a handful of varieties for its major crops. For example, in the U.S. two decades ago, 60 to 70% of the total bean acreage was planted with two to three bean varieties, 72% of the potato acreage with four varieties, and 53% with three cotton varieties. Researchers have repeatedly warned about the extreme vulnerability associated with this genetic uniformity. Perhaps the most striking example of vulnerability associated with homogenous uniform agriculture was the collapse of Irish potato production in 1845, where the uniform stock of potatoes was highly susceptible to the blight, Phytophthora infestans infestans. During the 19th century in France, wine grape production was wiped out by a virulent pest, Phylloxera vitifoliae, which eliminated 4 million hectares of uniform grape varieties. Banana monocultural plantations in Costa Rica have been repeatedly seriously jeopardized by diseases such as Fusarium oxysporum and yellow sigatoka. In the USA, in the early 1970s, uniform high-yielding maize hybrids comprised about 70% of all the maize varieties; a 15% loss of the entire crop by leaf blight occurred in that decade. A worrisome trend is the recent expansion of transgenic maize and soybean monoculture mostly grown in the US which has reached about 45 million hectares in less than 6 years.

Modern agroecosystems are unstable, and breakdowns manifest themselves as recurrent pest outbreaks in most cropping systems. The worsening of most pest problems has been experimentally linked to the expansion of crop monoculture at the expense of vegetation diversity. This diversity is a key landscape component providing crucial ecological services to ensure crop protection through provision of habitat and resources to natural pest enemies. Ninety-one percent of the 1.5 billion hectares of cropland worldwide are annual crops and are planted with mostly monocultures of wheat, rice, maize, cotton, and soybeans. One of the main problems arising from the homogenization of agricultural systems is an increased vulnerability of crops to insect pests and diseases, which can be devastating if they infest a uniform crop, especially in large plantations. To protect these crops, copious amounts of increasingly less effective and selective pesticides are injected into the biosphere at considerable environmental and human costs. These are clear signs that the pesticide-based approach to pest control has reached its limits. An alternative approach is needed; one based on the use of ecological principles in order to design more sustainable farming systems that take full advantage of the benefits of biodiversity in agriculture.

The Expansion of Monoculture Agriculture

Today, monoculture has increased dramatically worldwide, mainly through the geographical expansion of land devoted to single crops and year-to-year production of the same crop species on the same land. Available data indicate that the amount of crop diversity per unit of arable land has decreased and that croplands have shown a tendency toward concentration. There are political and economic forces influencing the trend to devote large areas to monoculture and, in fact, such systems are rewarded by economies of scale and contribute significantly to the ability of national agricultures to serve international markets.

The technologies which have facilitated the shift toward monoculture are mechanization, the improvement of crop varieties, and the development of agrochemicals to fertilize crops and control weeds and pests. Government commodity policies these past several decades have also encouraged the acceptance and utilization of these technologies. As a result, farms today are fewer, larger, more specialized and more capital-intensive. At the regional level, the increase in monoculture farming has meant that the entire agricultural support infrastructure (i.e. research, extension, suppliers, storage, transport, markets, etc.) has become more specialized.

From an ecological perspective, the regional consequences of monoculture specialization are many-fold:

- Most large-scale agricultural systems exhibit a poorly structured assemblage of farm components, with almost no linkages or complementary relationships between crop enterprises and among soils, crops and animals.

- Cycles of nutrients, energy, water and wastes have become more open, rather than closed as in a natural ecosystem. Despite the substantial amount of crop residues and manure produced in farms, it is becoming increasingly difficult to recycle nutrients, even within agricultural systems. Animal wastes cannot economically be returned to the land in a nutrient-recycling process because production is geographically remote from other systems which would complete the cycle. In many areas, agricultural waste has become a liability rather than a resource. Recycling of nutrients from urban centers back to the fields is similarly difficult.

- Part of the instability and susceptibility to pests of agroecosystems can be linked to the adoption of vast crop monocultures, which have concentrated resources for specialist crop herbivores and have increased the areas available for immigration of pests. This simplification has also reduced environmental opportunities for natural enemies. Consequently, pest outbreaks often occur with the simultaneous occurrence of large numbers of immigrant pests, inhibited populations of beneficial insects, favorable weather and vulnerable crop stages.

- As specific crops are expanded beyond their "natural" ranges or favorable regions to areas of high pest potential, or with limited water or low-fertility soils, intensified chemical controls are required to overcome such limiting factors. The assumption is that human intervention and the level of energy inputs that allow these expansions can be sustained indefinitely.

- Commercial farmers witness a constant parade of new crop varieties as varietal replacement due to biotic stresses and market changes has accelerated to unprecedented levels. A cultivar with improved disease or insect resistance makes a debut, performs well for a few years (typically 5-9 years) and is then succeeded by another variety when yields begin to slip, productivity is threatened, or a more promising cultivar becomes available. A variety's trajectory is characterized by a take-off phase when it is adopted by farmers, a middle stage when the planted area stabilizes, and finally a retraction of its acreage. Thus, stability in modern agriculture hinges on a continuous supply of new cultivars rather than a patchwork quilt of many different varieties planted on the same farm.

- The need to subsidize monoculture requires increases in the use of pesticides and fertilizers, but the efficiency of use of applied inputs is decreasing and crop yields in most key crops are leveling off. In some places, yields are actually in decline. There are different opinions as to the underlying causes of this phenomenon. Some believe that yields are leveling off because the maximum yield potential of current varieties is being approached, and therefore genetic engineering must be applied to the task of redesigning crops. Agroecologists, on the other hand, believe that the leveling off is because of the steady erosion of the productive base of agriculture through unsustainabie practices. . . .

The First Wave of Environmental Problems

The specialization of production units has led to the image that agriculture is a modern miracle of food production. Evidence indicates, however, that excessive reliance on monoculture farming and agro-industrial inputs, such as capital-intensive technology, pesticides, and chemical fertilizers, has negatively impacted the environment and rural society. Most agriculturalists had assumed that the agroecosystem/natural ecosystem dichotomy need not lead to undesirable consequences, yet, unfortunately, a number of "ecological diseases" have been associated with the intensification of food production. . . .

The bountiful harvests created . . . through the use of chemical fertilizers have associated, and often hidden, costs.

The loss of yields due to pests (reaching about 20-30% in most crops), despite the substantial increase in the use of pesticides (about 500 million kg of active ingredient worldwide) is [also] a symptom of the environmental crisis affecting agriculture. It is well known that cultivated plants grown in genetically homogenous monocultures do not possess the necessary ecological defense mechanisms to tolerate the impact of outbreaking pest populations. Modern agriculturists have selected crops for high yields and high palatability, making them more susceptible to pests by sacrificing natural resistance for productivity. On the other hand, modern agricultural practices negatively affect pest natural enemies, which in turn do not find the necessary environmental resources and opportunities in monocultures to effectively suppress pests by natural biological means. The lack of natural pest control mechanisms in monocultures makes modern agroecosystems heavily dependent on pesticides. In the U.S. approximately 500,000 tons of 600 different types of pesticides are used annually at a cost of $4.1 billion. The indirect costs of pesticide use to the environment and public health have to be balanced against their benefits. Based on the available data, the environmental costs (impacts on wildlife, pollinators, natural enemies, fisheries, water and development of resistance) and social costs (human poisonings and illnesses) of pesticide use reach about $8 billion each year. What is worrisome is that pesticide use is on the rise. Data from California shows that from 1941 to 1995, pesticide use increased from 161 to 212 million pounds of active ingredient. These increases were not due to increases in planted acreage, as statewide crop acreage remained constant during this period. Crops such as strawberries and grapes account for much of this increased use, which includes toxic pesticides, many of which are linked to cancers. On top of this, more than 500 species of arthropods have developed resistance against more than 1000 different types of pesticides which have been rendered useless to chemically control such pests.

Fertilizers, on the other hand, have been praised as being closely associated with the increase in food production observed in many countries. National average rates of nitrate applied to most arable lands fluctuate between 120-550 kg N/ha [kilograms of nitrate per hectare]. But the bountiful harvests created at least in part through the use of chemical fertilizers have associated, and often hidden, costs. A primary reason why chemical fertilizers pollute the environment is due to wasteful application and the fact that crops use them inefficiently. The fertilizer that is not recovered by the crop ends up in the environment, mostly in surface water or in groundwater. Nitrate contamination of aquifers is widespread and at dangerously high levels in many rural regions of the world. In the U.S., it is estimated that more than 25% of the drinking water wells contain nitrate levels above the 45 parts per million safety standard. Such nitrate levels are hazardous to human health, and studies have linked nitrate uptake to methaemoglobinemia in children and to gastric, bladder and oesophageal cancers in adults.

Fertilizer nutrients that enter surface waters (rivers, lakes, bays, etc.) can promote eutrophication, characterized initially by a population explosion of photosynthetic algae. Algal blooms turn the water bright green, prevent light from penetrating beneath surface layers, and therefore kill plants living on the bottom. Such dead vegetation serve as food for other aquatic microorganisms which soon deplete water of its oxygen, inhibiting the decomposition of organic residues, which accumulate on the bottom. Eventually, such nutrient enrichment of freshwater ecosystems leads to the destruction of all animal life in the water systems. In the US it is estimated that about 50-70% of all nutrients that reach surface waters is derived from fertilizers. Chemical fertilizers can also become air pollutants, and have recently been implicated in the destruction of the ozone layer and in global warming. Their excessive use has also been linked to the acidification/salinization of soils and to a higher incidence of insect pests and diseases through mediation of negative nutritional changes in crop plants. . . .

The Second Wave of Environmental Problems

Despite the fact that awareness of the impacts of modern technologies on the environment has increased, as we have traced pesticides in food chains and crop nutrients in streams and aquifers, there are those who still argue for further intensification to meet the requirements of agricultural production. It is in this context that supporters of "status-quo agriculture" celebrate the emergence of biotechnology as the latest magic bullet that will revolutionize agriculture with products based on nature's own methods, making farming more environmentally friendly and more profitable for the farmer. Clearly, certain forms of non-transformational biotechnology hold promise for an improved agriculture. However, given its present orientation and control by multinational corporations, it holds more promise for environmental harm, for the further industrialization of agriculture, and for the intrusion of private interests too far into public interest sector research.

What is ironic is the fact that the biorevolution is being brought forward by the same interests (such as Monsanto, Novartis, DuPont, etc.) that promoted the first wave of agrochemically-based agriculture. By equipping each crop with new "insecticidal genes," they are now promising the world safer pesticides, reduction of chemically-intensive farming and a more sustainable agriculture. As long as transgenic crops follow closely the pesticide paradigm, however, such biotechnological products will do nothing but reinforce the pesticide treadmill in agroecosystems, thus legitimizing the concerns that many scientists have expressed regarding the possible environmental risks of genetically engineered organisms.

Biotechnology Is a Threat to Biodiversity

David Kennell

David Kennell is professor emeritus of the Department of Molecular Microbiology at Washington University School of Medicine in St. Louis, Missouri.

Transgenic crops [crops that have genetic material from another species] will greatly accelerate the decline of biodiversity in the plant world. Reason: Seed corporations demand farmers buy seed from them each year—replacing the millennial practice of farmers selecting seeds best suited for their specific environments. By coercing governments of developing countries to plant genetically modified (GM) crops, much of the native crops are replaced by a monoculture of the GM crop for export to meet the country's debt.

The country then has to import food to replace their native crops. Once GM plants are introduced, farmers may be unable to grow non-GM crops. The Percy Schmeiser case in Saskatchewan, Canada has dramatized what is occurring on farms all over the world. The unintended spread of glyphosate-resistant pollen from Round-up Ready (RR) canola plants (possibly by wind, birds, trucks, etc.) contaminated Schmeiser's non-GM canola fields. Even though the court agreed that he never planted or wanted Monsanto's GM seeds, it ruled that he had to pay a huge patent fee to Monsanto.

This experience was not unique. The University of Manitoba found that 32 of the 33 commercially available seed lots of native canola have been contaminated with RR seeds. The canola of the Great Plains is rapidly becoming a monoculture

David Kennell, "Genetically Engineered Plant Crops: Potential for Disaster," *Synthesis/Regeneration*, vol. 35, fall 2004, pp. 10–11. Copyright © 2004 WD Press. Reproduced by permission.

variety, which carries the potential for disaster. The RR plants have even invaded other crop species—becoming a "super-weed."

The Importance of Plant Diversity

Why is biodiversity important? The great Russian botanist Nikolai Vavilov traveled the world collecting and categorizing plants and seeds. He proposed that there are eight centers of origin of the major species of food plants, all in Third World countries, e.g., corn, Mexico; rice, India; Andes mountains, potatoes, tomatoes; China, soybeans. There have been dozens of major crop disasters in our world in the last 150 years following the great potato blight famine in Ireland in the 1840s. A few examples:

- 1870s: coffee rust in Ceylon, India, East Asia, Africa (the reason England is a nation of tea drinkers).

- 1890s: cotton epidemic.

- 1904, 1916, 1954: stem rust in US wheat (75% of wheat lost in 1954).

- 1940s: brown spot disease of Indian rice (Bengal famine).

- 1940s and again in 1950s: 80% of US oat crop.

- 1940s: USSR wheat crop; led to huge Russian grain deal.

- 1970s: corn blight (Bipolaris) in US destroyed 15% of corn crop.

- 1980: French grapes; aphid powdery mildew (France turned to the US for resistant germplasm).

- 1990s: Russet Burbank potato (Phytophthora infestans blight) is high in mass/water (the reason it is used for McDonalds fries); the blight spread over the world.

Each time resistance was needed. Each time it was most likely found in centers of origin in land races that had escaped "homogenization." Vavilov observed: "These centers are also centers of greatest diversity of varieties and also a rich source of genetic alleles [gene variations] for resistance to specific crop diseases, having evolved varieties during millions of years through many different environments and diseases."

There is a good chance GM agriculture will lead to cata-strophic famine in the world by greatly decreasing the gene pool of plants.

For example, a worthless-looking primordial wheat plant from Turkey is the primitive progenitor in all breeding pro-grams for US wheat. By 1984, 58% of US wheat used original germplasm—it was only 7% in 1969.

Consequences of GM Plants

GM plants disrupt the normal ecology selected in millions of years of evolution with some unknown and some known con-sequences. The incorporated foreign resistance genes provide only short-term advantage. Nature selects for strains resistant to them. Resistance to Round-up is increasing: goosegrass in Malaysia, Italian ryegrass, Australian ryegrass, horseweed in US. Now, over 500 species are resistant to pesticides and over 100 weed species are resistant to herbicides. Pesticide use is up more than 1000 fold on corn since 1945 but corn crop losses increased from 3.5% to 12% in the same period of time.

Concurrently, many beneficial insects and microorganisms are killed by the pesticides, and by the added "inerts" that ac-count for most of their bulk (they are not identified even though many are toxic). Bt toxin from engineered plants is much more stable than the natural toxin from *B. thuringiensis*. It can remain potent for months in the soil. A teaspoon of soil contains millions of bacteria and fungi, as well as arthropods and earthworms. Soil is a living environment that is unique for each specific place on the planet after millions of years of evolution. It is estimated that one inch of topsoil took 500 years to evolve.

Solutions

Return to the practice of crop rotation. In 1945 corn was grown in rotation with soybeans, wheat and other crops. Corn on corn (increased with GM agriculture) promotes survival of disease vectors and weeds specific for corn. Also, there is increased water runoff and soil erosion. Data for cases where yields have been reduced from GM crops compared to non-GM crops are accumulating. Also, rotation provides more home-grown food and self-sufficiency.

The United Nations World Food Program concluded that there is 1.5 times the food needed to feed all people. Hunger is a problem of food distribution and of returning land to native farming. GM-crops have nothing to do with solving hunger; in fact, there is a good chance GM agriculture will lead to catastrophic famine in the world by greatly decreasing the gene pool of plants and by major disruption of the ecology of life that has evolved over millions of years. Foreign genes inserted at random sites automatically cause two or more unknown mutations in a host genome, creating unknown phenotypes.

The only purpose of ... GM plants is to control the world's food supply and thus guarantee ... profits for the multinational agrichemical corporations.

No one knows the consequences of hundreds of man-made life forms being spread across our planet! It is a completely uncontrolled experiment that has no boundaries.

The only purpose of the promotion of GM plants is to control the world's food supply and thus guarantee continuing and increasing profits for the multinational agrichemical corporations.

Overfishing Is the Biggest Threat to Marine Biodiversity

United Nations Environment Programme

The United Nations Environment Programme (UNEP) is a United Nations organization that encourages nations to care for the environment.

Despite its crucial importance for the survival of humanity, marine biodiversity is in ever-greater danger, with the depletion of fisheries among biggest concerns.

The Problem of Overfishing

Fishing is central to the livelihood and food security of 200 million people, especially in the developing world, while one of five people on this planet depends on fish as the primary source of protein. According to UN [United Nations] agencies, aquaculture—the farming and stocking of aquatic organisms including fish, molluscs, crustaceans and aquatic plants—is growing more rapidly than all other animal food producing sectors. But amid facts and figures about aquaculture's soaring worldwide production rates, other, more sobering, statistics reveal that global main marine fish stocks are in jeopardy, increasingly pressured by overfishing and environmental degradation.

"Overfishing cannot continue," warned Nitin Desai, Secretary General of the 2002 World Summit on Sustainable Development, which took place in Johannesburg. "The depletion of fisheries poses a major threat to the food supply of millions of people." The Johannesburg Plan of Implementation calls for the establishment of Marine Protected Areas (MPAs), which many experts believe may hold the key to conserving and

United Nations Environment Programme (UNEP), "Overfishing: A Threat to Marine Biodiversity," www.un.org, 2004. Reproduced by permission of United Nations Environment Programme (UNEP), Kenya.

boosting fish stocks. Yet, according to the UN Environment Programme's (UNEP) World Conservation Monitoring Centre, in Cambridge, UK, less than one per cent of the world's oceans and seas are currently in MPAs.

Only a multinational approach can counterbalance the rate of depletion of the world's fisheries.

The magnitude of the problem of overfishing is often overlooked, given the competing claims of deforestation, desertification, energy resource exploitation and other biodiversity depletion dilemmas. The rapid growth in demand for fish and fish products is leading to fish prices increasing faster than prices of meat. As a result, fisheries investments have become more attractive to both entrepreneurs and governments, much to the detriment of small-scale fishing and fishing communities all over the world. In the last decade, in the north Atlantic region, commercial fish populations of cod, hake, haddock and flounder have fallen by as much as 95%, prompting calls for urgent measures. Some are even recommending zero catches to allow for regeneration of stocks, much to the ire of the fishing industry.

Urgent Action Needed

According to a Food and Agriculture Organization (FAO) estimate, over 70% of the world's fish species are either fully exploited or depleted. The dramatic increase of destructive fishing techniques worldwide destroys marine mammals and entire ecosystems. FAO reports that illegal, unreported and unregulated fishing worldwide appears to be increasing as fishermen seek to avoid stricter rules in many places in response to shrinking catches and declining fish stocks. Few, if any, developing countries and only a limited number of developed ones are on track to put into effect by this year the International Plan of Action to Prevent, Deter and Eliminate

Unreported and Unregulated Fishing. Despite the fact that each region has its Regional Sea Conventions, and some 108 governments and the European Commission have adopted the UNEP Global Programme of Action for the Protection of the Marine Environment from Land based Activities, oceans are cleared at twice the rate of forests.

The Johannesburg forum stressed the importance of restoring depleted fisheries and acknowledged that sustainable fishing requires partnerships by and between governments, fishermen, communities and industry. It urged countries to ratify the Convention on the Law of the Sea and other instruments that promote maritime safety and protect the environment from marine pollution and environmental damage by ships. Only a multilateral approach can counterbalance the rate of depletion of the world's fisheries which has increased more than four times in the past 40 years.

High-Yield, Industrial Agriculture Protects Biodiversity

Center for Global Food Issues

Center for Global Food Issues is a project of the Hudson Institute, a nonpartisan research organization that conducts research and analysis of agriculture and the environmental concerns surrounding food and fiber production.

On April 30, 2002, a broad coalition of food, environmental, farming and forestry experts—including two Nobel Peace Prize laureates—invited their colleagues worldwide to co-sign a declaration in favor of high-yield conservation. Their message was simple: "Growing more crops and trees per acre leaves more land for Nature," said Dr. Norman Borlaug, 1970 Nobel Peace Prize laureate and father of the Green Revolution. "We cannot choose between feeding malnourished children and saving endangered wild species. Without higher yields, peasant farmers will destroy the wildlands and species to keep their children from starving. Sustainably higher yields of crops and trees are the only visible way to save both."

Misconceptions

According to Dr. Patrick Moore, co-founder of Greenpeace, "There's a misconception that it would be better to go back to more primitive methods of agriculture because chemicals are bad or genetics is bad. This is not true. We need to use the science and technology we have developed in order to feed the world's population, a growing population. And the more yield we get per acre of land the less nature has to be destroyed to do that ... It's simple arithmetic. The more people there are,

Center for Global Food Issues, "High-yield Conservation Protects Biodiversity," www.highyieldconservation.org, July 19, 2007. Reproduced by permission.

the more forest has to be cleared to feed them, and the only way to offset that is to have more yield per acre."

"The solutions that are being offered by the environmentalist movement are quite often in total opposition to the objectives that we are trying to achieve: protection of the environment and feeding people," said co-signer Eugène Lapointe, President of the World Conservation Trust. "Most environmentalist movements, most organizations, are not solution oriented—they are drama, they are scandal oriented. The Center for Global Food Issues, in its initiative called High-yield Farming and Forestry, is probably the best example of how we can achieve true innovative and practical solutions. The major objective that all of us should have is feeding people while protecting the waters and the lands that we have."

Organic Farming Could Lead to Deforestation

"Two years ago in Britain, the Cooperative Wholesale Association, which farms both organically and conventionally, said they get 44% less wheat per acre from their organic fields. If that's the right number, Europe—to feed itself, not to export, just to feed itself today—would need additional crop land equal to all of the forest area in Germany, France, Denmark, and the UK," said Dennis Avery, director of the Center for Global Food Issues. Added Dr. Borlaug, "We aren't going to feed 6 billion people with organic fertilizer. If we tried to do it, we would level most of our forest and many of those lands would be productive only for a short period of time."

Other initial signers of the declaration included:

- Oscar Arias, Nobel Peace Prize winner and Former President of Costa Rica

- Per Pinstrup-Andersen, 2001 World Food Prize winner and Director of the International Food Policy Research Institute

- James Lovelock, Independent Scientist, author of *The Gaia Hypothesis*

- Rudy Boschwitz, former US Senator and advisory chair at the Center for Global Food Issues

- George McGovern, former US Senator and UN "Ambassador to the Hungry"

They have since been joined by over 800 people from over 50 countries who have signed in support.

Biotechnology Is Not a Threat to Biodiversity

Michael Howie

Michael Howie is the managing editor of Feedstuffs, *a weekly newspaper that provides news and analysis of issues relating to agribusiness and food production.*

It is a myth that the introduction of plants derived from biotechnology will lower biodiversity around the world, said Dr. Klaus Ammann at BIO 2003 [a gathering of biotech leaders] ... [on] June 24 [2003].

Ammann, director of the botanical garden at the University of Bern, Switzerland, said biotechnology can actually improve and protect biodiversity by not only saving land but by using that diversity to improve agriculture in the long-term. Still, he said, the precautionary approach to biotechnology in some parts of the world tend[s] to mislead and misreport the facts. "Scientists should come out of their box and talk with the public and fight 'corporate antagonists' like Greenpeace," he said.

Ammana said some plants have been bombarded with radiation in order to change the genomes, "which seems more like 'frankenfoods' to me," but that hasn't seemed to rile antibiotech groups. As for gene flow, Ammann said pollen did not just learn to fly when genetically modified crops were developed. "It's been flying forever," he said, adding that geneflow is the basis for evolution and varies widely from year to year. It is easy to do charts and such to see how far pollen flows, he said, but that doesn't necessarily mean anything because of all the variables and complexity of the subject.

Biodiversity Study

In a study on the subject, Ammann said biodiversity encompasses the fundamental basis of life on earth, including genetic, species and ecosystem diversity. Generally, he said, there is a need to better understand biodiversity in terms of its fundamental components (genes and taxa), the interrelatedness of these components (ecology), their importance for human life and life in general and the factors that threaten biodiversity.

Increasing human population and limited arable land have demanded increased agricultural productivity.

Biodiversity on Earth is concentrated in unmanaged habitats within the tropics, he said, while in temperate zones, particularly in the European Union, almost 50% of the landscape is agricultural, and agricultural lands contain a significant portion of the biodiversity in such zones. Therefore, he said, the greatest threats to biodiversity are destruction and deterioration of habitats, particularly in tropical developing countries, and introductions of exotic species. Maintaining biodiversity requires addressing these threats.

Biodiversity and Agriculture

Many of the factors affecting biodiversity are related directly or indirectly to the needs of agricultural production, and it is important to consider how these impacts could be mitigated, he said. Increasing human population and limited arable land have demanded increased agricultural productivity leading to more intensive agricultural practices on a global basis. In response, higher yielding crop varieties have been coupled with increased inputs in the form of fertilizers and pesticides and more intensive practices such as greater tillage of soil.

More recently, though, biotech crops with insect resistance and herbicide tolerance have . . . demonstrated the potential to enhance productivity. These technologies have been broadly adopted in some parts of the world and have reduced the dependence of broad-spectrum insecticides in some systems and reduced how often land is tilled in others.

Ammann said agricultural impacts on biodiversity can be divided into two sectors: in-field biodiversity and natural (off-site) biodiversity. Intensive agriculture has a negative effect on both species and genetic biodiversity within agricultural systems, primarily because of low crop and structural diversity but also through pesticide use and tillage, he said. These impacts can be addressed by encouraging diversification of agricultural systems and by reducing broad-spectrum insecticide and tillage, both of which biotech crops can achieve in some systems.

The development . . . of biotech crop varieties does not seem to represent any greater risk to crop genetic diversity than [conventional] breeding programs.

Agricultural impacts on natural biodiversity primarily stem from conversion of natural habitats into agricultural production, he said. The transport of fertilizers and pesticides into aquatic systems also cause significant habitat deterioration through eutrophication [over-enrichment of water with nutrients such as nitrogen], he said. Increasing the efficiency of agricultural production can reduce these impacts, as can minimizing off-site movement of fertilizers and pesticides by reducing tillage and total agricultural inputs. Technologies such as biotech crops are important in this respect, he said.

Overall, creating agricultural systems with minimal impact on biodiversity will require utilizing all available technologies while simultaneously encouraging appropriate farmer practices.

Environmentalists' Exaggerations

Still, he [Ammann] said, some green groups have taken scientific lab studies and exaggerated the results for their benefits. For example, he said, previous reports indicating the hazard of Bt corn pollen to monarch butterflies are "inadequate to assess risk, because assigning risk can be accomplished only when the likelihood of toxic response can be properly expressed and the likelihood of exposure is estimated through appropriate observations."

As part of the study, Ammann used a comprehensive set of new data and a formalized approach to risk assessment that integrates aspects of exposure to characterize the risk posed to monarchs from Bt corn pollen. Characterization of acute toxic effects alone indicates that the potential for hazard to monarchs is currently restricted to certain hybrids (Bt event 176), which express Cry 1Ab protein in pollen at a level sufficient to show measurable effects. Event 176 hybrids have always had a minor presence in the corn market, and current plantings are rapidly declining.

"What really counts in growing biotech crops is the actual toxicity impact under field conditions, and this impact has been shown to be negligible," he said, yet groups continue to cite early research that has been proven to be an unreliable analysis of "real world" conditions, as demonstrated by other research.

Ammann also noted that preserving the genetic diversity in crops—biotech or not—is important but is being addressed by various public and private programs. "In this respect, biotechnology can be a valuable tool for introducing novel genes or valuable genes from old cultivars," he said.

In conclusion, he said the development and introduction of biotech crop varieties does not seem to represent any greater risk to crop genetic diversity than breeding programs associated with conventional agriculture. "The view, published by the National Research Council in 1989, that biotech crops offer more precision in lab and field testing than conventional ones has not been disproven to date," he said.

Commercial Fishing Is Not Significantly Affecting the Oceans' Biodiversity

Jerry Fraser

Jerry Fraser, a fisherman for more than seven years, is the editor of National Fisherman, *an industry trade magazine.*

Most of you have by now heard the uproar following the publication of research in the Nov[ember] 3 [2006] journal *Science* suggesting that loss of biodiversity has drastic impacts on marine ecosystems. The report, authored by Boris Worm of Nova Scotia's Dalhousie University, among others, concludes that, given the "ongoing erosion of diversity" the "global collapse" of commercially fished species will occur by 2048.

No way *USA Today* could pass up this front-page news. "Oversight of commercial fishing must be strengthened or there may eventually be no more seafood," wrote reporter Elizabeth Weise, leading the charge for mainstream publications from coast to coast that routinely demonize commercial fishing. It's one thing to jump to a conclusion; it's quite another, as Weise has, to jump over it.

A More Nuanced Vision of Marine Biodiversity

Worm and his cohorts have assembled data that suggest to them that biodiversity is an asset in marine ecosystems, a conclusion I suspect most of us have long since arrived at, via intuition if not observation. They lay out the consequences, near as they can figure, if we fritter biodiversity away.

But where *USA Today*, and no doubt others, sees only factory trawlers and men in oilskins, Worm and others have a much more nuanced vision. "Changes in marine diversity," they write, "are directly caused by exploitation, pollution, and habitat destruction, or indirectly through climate change and related perturbations of ocean biogeochemistry." This is the crucial point. It is all well and good for *USA Today* and others to lay all that is wrong with our oceans at the feet of commercial fishing, but clearly exploitation is but one of several factors that must be considered when modeling marine ecosystems. Moreover, of all these factors, commercial fishing—this country in particular—is by any measure subject to the most control, and going forward, is likely to produce fewest adverse impacts.

Whatever our past sins, the U.S. fishing industry in the last decade has emerged as a true steward of the [marine] resource.

Clearly we will continue to regulate fishing, but let's be candid. The U.S. commercial fleet is but a fraction of its former size. Our gear is more selective every season, and although habitat impacts from fishing gear have yet to be quantified, other than by emotional exhortation, the industry has embraced the goal of reducing friction across the sea floor.

And the fact is, terms like "overfished" and "depleted," while suggesting that a species is being overharvested, refer only to the biomass of a stock versus an historical benchmark. A stock subject to little or even no harvesting is often classified as overfished or depleted, leaving the public and uninformed reporters to conclude that rapacious fishermen are plundering away.

Meanwhile, we flush millions of tons of fertilizer and other agricultural runoff through our rivers into the sea and develop our coastlines far beyond the ability of residual terrain to absorb runoff. We build power plants and other facilities that simmer seawater with their outfalls. No one may know for certain what is going on with rising temperatures in various places around the world, but we can observe their effects on polar icecaps and in some of our oceans' most prodigious currents. And of course, we continue to flirt with the catastrophic consequences of oil spills.

So as it happens, we in the U.S. fishing industry know exactly what Worm and his fellow researchers are trying to say. We may lack the wherewithal to say whether time will run out in 2048, but we know the clock is ticking.

The Solution Is Not a Fishing Ban

It is high time our fellow Americans (and for that matter, the citizens and governments of the world) stopped deluding themselves with the notion that if commercial fishing would somehow disappear, the oceans would bloom with primeval abundance. Whatever our past sins, the U.S. fishing industry in the last decade has emerged as a true steward of the resource. But it is not in our power, or Boris Worm's, for that matter, to be the ultimate steward of the resource. That is the challenge for an enlightened society with the resolve to make crucial decisions about the way it interacts with the oceans. It's a free country, and we can make these decisions or not. But focus only on commercial fishing and whenever 2048 arrives, it will be sooner than you think.

CHAPTER 4

How Can the Earth's Biodiversity Be Preserved?

Chapter Preface

For most of the history of the world, the vast majority of the Earth was truly a wilderness in which humans had yet to leave their mark. However, beginning in the 1800s, the start of the industrial age, many people became increasingly concerned about how to protect the natural environment from human activities. In the United States, one of the first actions taken to preserve the country's natural treasures was the creation of national parks. The first National Park to be established was Yellowstone in 1872, and in the early 1900s President Theodore Roosevelt, a great lover of the outdoors, designated five other national parks along with numerous wildlife refuges. In the early 2000s, the national park system protects 391 regions covering 83 million acres and wildlife refuges protect 547 areas covering another 93 million acres.

Another initiative undertaken in the late 1800s was the national forest system. This designation was created to protect watersheds and forests during an age of rampant logging. As of 2008, the system includes 155 forest regions covering 187 acres, and it is managed for multiple uses, including recreation, river and stream protection, as well as some highly controversial commercial logging.

Wilderness preservation again became popular in the 1960s, when environmentalists began drawing attention to the damage being done to the environment by human activities such as industry and agriculture, which caused widespread water, air, and soil pollution. During this period, another piece of landmark legislation, the Wilderness Act of 1964, was enacted to give permanent protection to some of the remaining natural wilderness regions. Under the act, a wilderness region is generally considered to be an area that has not been significantly changed by humans; it is specifically defined as follows: "[an] area where the earth and its community of life are untrammeled by man, where man himself is a visitor who does not remain. . . . Federal land retaining its primeval character and influence, without permanent improvements or human habitation." The act gave Congress the authority to designate wilderness areas and to manage them to preserve their natural condition. Generally, mechanized transportation (such as cars, snowmobiles, and bikes) and commercial timber or mining operations are prohibited in these areas, but visitors are permitted to ski, hunt, fish, hike, kayak, and enjoy similar non-mechanized recreational activities. As of 2008, approximately 100 million acres have been designated as wilderness in the United States. Wilderness areas covered by the act include regions in all but six states—everything from southern swamps to hardwood forests in the northeast and deserts in the southwest. Almost half of this wilderness acreage, however, is found in Alaska.

While private lands are increasingly developed for housing and commercial purposes, the national parks and federally designated wilderness areas protect some of the last remaining areas of natural biodiverity in the United States. Experts say they offer an oasis of survival for thousands of species, including about 400 endangered or threatened species. For example, species such as wolves at Yellowstone, coho salmon at Point Reyes National Seashore, and sea lions at Channel Islands National Park depend on the park areas for their survival.

Yet even these protected areas are under assault today. Many of these parks or wilderness areas are not large enough to survive in isolation as healthy ecosystems and many are threatened as development edges closer and closer, eliminating habitat next to their boundaries. Similarly, these parks and wild areas often depend on natural systems such as free-flowing rivers, naturally occurring fires, erosion, and storms; however, human attempts to divert or suppress nature outside or near the parks can have unintended, devastating effects within protected areas. In addition, many invasive, non-native plants and animals have been introduced or spread inside these protected regions, sometimes causing disruptions to the original ecosystems. Of course, one identified threat is global warming, which may dramatically change temperatures and conditions within protected areas in ways that may be destructive to wildlife and native vegetation.

To help preserve biodiversity in U.S. public parks and wilderness areas, environmentalists urge that efforts be made to fight invasive species, to protect endangered wildlife, to halt and reverse human development activities that cause creeping habitat destruction, and to enlarge park and wilderness areas to encompass some neighboring ecosystems. Protecting biodiversity in these publicly owned areas in the United States is difficult, but the challenge is even greater in the even-more-threatened private areas both in the United States and around the world. The authors of the viewpoints included in this chapter pose a variety of suggestions for preserving biodiversity on a more global scale.

Conservation Efforts Should Target Biodiversity "Hotspots"

Peter A. Seligmann

Peter A. Seligmann is chairman and CEO of Conservation International, a U.S.-based nonprofit organization that works to protect the richest regions of plant and animal diversity and biodiversity wilderness around the globe.

In recent decades, much of the natural world has been under continuous assault on an unprecedented scale. Mighty rivers are reduced to a trickle by ill-conceived dam projects. Animals are trapped, killed, and exported alive to feed an insatiable trade in everything from bush meat to exotic pets. Half of the world's tropical rain forests, nature's repository for the richest collections of terrestrial plant and animal species, have been destroyed for lumber and for development projects, many unsustainable. The oceans have been plundered by giant industrial fishing fleets to the point where 70 percent of commercial species are over-fished, and 90 per cent of top marine predators like cod, tuna, swordfish, and shark have disappeared.

Targeting Hotspots

Tackling a problem of this scale and complexity, often with modest funds, means that conservationists must be able to pinpoint the places where the greatest conservation gains can be made with the wisest investments. This requires the close study and protection of regions that support the richest varieties of plant and animal species, and also face the greatest threats. Of particular concern are those species that are en-

Peter A. Seligmann, "The Planet Faces a Biodiversity Crisis," *Earth Focus One Planet-One Community*, vol. 29, spring 2006. Copyright © 2006 Old City Publishing, Inc. Reproduced by permission.

demic or native to an area—plants or creatures found nowhere else on Earth and therefore, irreplaceable if lost.

Conservation International (CI) has identified 34 hotspots, places so abundant in biodiversity that they warrant the highest level of protection. More than 800 CI scientists, economists, anthropologists, and other experts—many of them foreign nationals—work in more than 40 countries to safeguard these ecological crown jewels that circle the globe from the tropical Andes to the mountains of Southwest China. In many cases, CI works closely with indigenous peoples to help them protect their lands that are part of these special places.

Nature's Emergency Room

The remaining intact portions of these 34 biodiversity hotspots today cover only 2.3 percent of the Earth's land surface, a little larger than the Indian sub-continent. In the pre-industrial era, they comprised 15.7 percent, about the size of the former USSR. Even so, these fragments harbor as many as 50 percent of all vascular plant species, and 42 percent of terrestrial vertebrate species, as endemics.

Hotspots are nature's emergency rooms where conservationists work to protect and restore to health the most critical patients.

To qualify as a hotspot, a region must have lost at least 70 percent of its original vegetation due to the impact of human activities. They must also hold at least 1500 endemic plant species because where there is high plant diversity, there is usually high animal diversity.

In a sense, hotspots are nature's emergency rooms where conservationists work to protect and restore to health the most critical patients. CI's reach, however, is far broader. We also work to preserve entire ecosystems that provide us with a vast array of benefits.

These "ecosystem services" sustain and enrich our lives. They include food, medicines, clean air and water, flood and climate control, energy and raw materials, soil regeneration, crop pollination, disease prevention, recreation, spiritual sustenance, and many others. By protecting ecosystems, CI helps to assure that these natural assets will continue to benefit humankind.

Today, the Earth is facing a biodiversity crisis—one that will affect everyone. In tandem with our partners in the global conservation movement, CI is engaging governments, corporations, funding institutions, indigenous groups, communities, and people everywhere, to set the course for a new age of global conservation and assure that future generations continue to reap the benefits that nature provides for us all.

Green Development Offers a Way to Save Biodiversity

Noel Castree

Noel Castree teaches in the School of Geography at the University of Manchester, in the United Kingdom.

What is green development? How does it work? And is it really an effective way to combine economic development with environmental protection?. . .

Green Development for the Developing World

In recent years, governments worldwide have been paying unprecedented attention to human use and abuse of the environment. A wave of new environmental problems—from global warming to the mass destruction of tropical rainforest—has led to increasing efforts to reduce the human impact on nature. However, for many countries environmental protection has, until recently, been seen as an unaffordable luxury.

Consider the following facts. In 1998 a mere 16% of the world's population enjoyed some 80% of its wealth and most of this 80% was concentrated in just a few countries. Given this degree of uneven development, poorer countries—particularly the so-called 'least developed nations'—simply cannot afford measures to protect nature. Indeed, it has been argued that for very poor Southern countries there is a fundamental contradiction between development and environmental protection.

On the one hand, poor nations such as Ethiopia desperately need economic development to help eradicate poverty, malnutrition and starvation. On the other, economic develop-

Noel Castree, "Green Development: Saving Nature by Selling It?" *Geography Review*, vol. 16, iss. 3, January 2003, p. 12. Copyright © 2003 Philip Allan Updates. Reproduced by permission.

ment typically entails major—and frequently harmful—transformations of the environment. Certainly, if one looks at the experience of the Northern countries, development has resulted in massive pollution and resource destruction.

The basic idea behind green development is that nature can pay for its own survival.

Is there a way past this environment-development contradiction for Southern nations? Some geographers and environmental managers think there is. Since the early 1990s the idea of 'green development' has become increasingly popular in development theory and practice, and is being promoted by many environmental policy makers working in the developing world.

Selling Nature in Order to Save It

The basic idea behind green development is that nature can pay for its own survival. As noted above, one of the reasons why states like Ethiopia have been reluctant to develop environmental protection programmes is that they are usually costly. For instance, protecting a large area of upland forest might be environmentally worthwhile. However, in economic and humanitarian terms it might be better to clear-cut the forest in order to provide fuel and shelter for a poor domestic population. The solution, some have argued, is to make environmental protection profitable so that it can contribute to rather than detract from the development process.

Thus, to take the case of the upland forest once again, the Ethiopian government might get the UK [United Kingdom] to pay 50 million [pounds sterling] over 20 years to prevent the forest being felled. Why would the UK do this? One reason is because burning wood is a major source of carbon dioxide, one of the chief causes of global warming. The UK has signed up to the global Climate Change Convention which aims to tackle global warming. Paying for the survival of an Ethiopian forest helps reduce world carbon dioxide emissions. At the same time it gives the Ethiopian government valuable foreign currency with which to further development among its needy population. In sum nature—in this case a forest—is sold to ensure its survival. At the same time, there is a development spin-off—in this case foreign currency. . . .

Green development is now big business. A number of developing countries have embraced the theory and put it into practice. Two of the most frequently mentioned examples are elephants in Kenya and biodiversity in the Central American country of Costa Rica. Let's examine these in turn to understand what green development looks like in practice.

Ecotourism in Kenya

Africa contains the majority of the world's elephants. In the 1970s there were around 1.3 million elephants roaming the continent. By 1989 their number had declined to just over half a million, mainly because of two things: ivory traders killing elephants for their tusks and local people killing elephants which trampled or ate their crops. In 1990 the 147 governments which were parties to the Convention on International Trade in Endangered Species (CITES) put elephants on their 'most endangered list' and stepped up attempts to protect the animals.

Kenya has been a lead player in this elephant conservation programme and currently [as of 2003] has a herd of some 29,000 animals. The herd recovery has been achieved using green development policies. Specifically, elephants have been protected by charging 'ecotourists'—usually westerners looking for a 'wildlife experience'—for access to them. These ecotourists fall into two main categories: 'passive' ecotourists who come to Kenya to see and photograph elephants and other wild animals; and 'pro-active' ecotourists who come as 'trophy hunters' to kill them. This latter form of ecotourism may seem to contradict the aim of protecting elephants! But the idea is that a minority of elephants (around 150) are sacrificed annually in order to pay for the protection of the wider herd.

Biodiversity Prospecting in Costa Rica

Costa Rica is one of the world's so-called 'biodiversity hotspots'. Biodiversity is a measure of the genetic and species variety within a given ecosystem. Costa Rica, as a tropical country, is teeming with plant, animal and insect life. It is believed that such biodiversity hotspots contain many as yet unknown species, which may one day be valuable for medical purposes, tourism or as resources. This is why, in 1993, the American pharmaceutical company Merck signed a 'biodiversity prospecting agreement' with the Costa Rican government. The idea was that, just as a gold prospector buys a plot of land in which to search for precious metal, Merck could buy the right to collect (or 'prospect for') samples of plants, animals and insects from all parts of Costa Rica. If those samples could, through scientific research and new genetic engineering techniques, be turned into valuable products, then Merck would be allowed to reap most of the commercial benefits.

Upon closer inspection the [green development] practice does not always live up to the twin aims of protecting nature and stimulating development.

Merck paid Costa Rica $1.1 million, one tenth of which went to the country's national park service (the Servicio de Parques Nacionales). In addition, one tenth of any royalties from products Merck develops using its Costa Rican samples will go back to Costa Rica. Just as ecotourism has helped pay for the survival of Kenyan elephants, so Costa Rica's agreement with Merck has helped pay for the protection of biodi-

versity. In both cases, nature has been sold or given an economic value in order to save it.

Evaluating Green Development

In both theory and practice green development appears flaw-
less in its logic and outcomes. By giving nature a price and
selling it in some way, sufficient revenue is generated both to
protect it and to encourage economic development among local communities. However, upon closer inspection the practice
does not always live up to the twin aims of protecting nature
and stimulating development. We can see this by revisiting the
Kenyan and Costa Rican examples, along with some others.

In Kenya the Kenya Wildlife Service (KWS) has been
plagued by corruption (a problem in many Kenyan
organisations). This means that much of the ecotourist money
generated from elephant watching and hunting has not actually trickled down to local communities. At the same time,
CITES has recently considered making the ivory trade legal
once again and this has already led to a rise in the poaching
of elephants for their tusks. Finally, Kenya's population has
tripled to 30 million since the 1960s, placing great demands
on land. Elephants which stray out of national parks and reserves are frequently shot because they trample crops. Local
people—aware of the corruption in the KWS and the money
to be made from ivory—are often unwilling to exercise re-
straint when elephants destroy their livelihood.

In Costa Rica too, a closer look at green development
policy shows how theory does not always translate well into
practice. First, the $1.1 million paid by Merck is a drop in the
ocean compared to how much Costa Rica will have to spend
in the future to protect its biodiversity. Second, very few local
people have benefited from the biodiversity prospecting agreement. In fact, Merck employed just 30 sample collectors—or
local 'parataxonomista' as they are called—at fairly low wages.
The bulk of the $1.1 million went into central government

coffers. Finally, in the southeast of Costa Rica there are many aboriginal groups who claim that the plant, animal and insect resources in the area belong to them and cannot be bought for money. But their rights have been ignored as samples have been taken back to Merck's US research laboratories with a view to developing profitable drugs from them.

In India difficulties in both monitoring and policing what happens to nature are undermining wildlife conservation programmes. For instance, India has just 3,800 tigers left in the wild, many of them protected in nature reserves as part of the country's Project Tiger. As with Kenya's elephants, the idea is that Western ecotourists 'on safari' can pay for the tigers' survival. However, there is a lucrative black market in tiger teeth, claws and genitals (China is the main destination for these). Consequently, poachers illegally kill tigers while the project wardens lack the resources effectively to watch over the vast areas where tigers roam.

Hard economic logic often dictates that it is more profitable to destroy nature than to conserve it.

Even more dramatic are the problems faced by Indonesia, which has the potential to become one of the world's major ecotourist destinations. Like Costa Rica it is a biodiversity hotspot and contains everything from orangutans and rhinos to pythons and rare parrots. But the country underwent a major economic crisis in 1998 in which its national currency became so devalued as to be virtually worthless. Desperate for valuable foreign currency with which to buy imported food and goods, many of the country's poorer people have been systematically raiding game parks and wildlife sanctuaries for wild animals, birds and insects. For instance, some turtle species are worth 100 [pounds sterling] per animal in Hong Kong (where they are a delicacy used for soup). It has been virtually impossible for Indonesia's national park service to prevent this mass pillaging of wildlife. At a time of economic austerity, the Indonesian government can ill afford to spend money on nature instead of people. . . .

An Uncertain Future

Green development theory promises much, but green development policies frequently fail to make these promises good. Hard economic logic often dictates that it is more profitable to destroy nature than to conserve it. This is, of course, a terribly shortsighted view. We cannot afford, on moral or economic grounds, to allow species to become extinct in the name of short-term profitability. But as the Indonesian case shows, we also need to find far greater incentives with which to encourage people in the developing world to protect their natural heritage. For radical environmentalists the only real solution is for the developed countries to inject enormous amounts of money into green development programmes in the South. Failing this, it seems that the moderate success enjoyed by some 'sell nature to save it' programmes will be eclipsed by an increasing number of failures.

The Convention on Biological Diversity Is Helping to Preserve Biodiversity

Secretariat of the Convention on Biological Diversity

Signed by 150 government leaders at the 1992 Rio Earth Summit, the Convention on Biological Diversity is dedicated to promoting sustainable development.

The rich tapestry of life on our planet is the outcome of over 3.5 billion years of evolutionary history. It has been shaped by forces such as changes in the planet's crust, ice ages, fire, and interaction among species. Now, it is increasingly being altered by humans. From the dawn of agriculture, some 10,000 years ago, through the Industrial Revolution of the past three centuries, we have reshaped our landscapes on an ever-larger and lasting scale. We have moved from hacking down trees with stone tools to literally moving mountains to mine the Earth's resources. Old ways of harvesting are being replaced by more intensive technologies, often without controls to prevent over-harvesting. For example, fisheries that have fed communities for centuries have been depleted in a few years by huge, sonar-guided ships using nets big enough to swallow a dozen jumbo jets at a time. By consuming ever more of nature's resources, we have gained more abundant food and better shelter, sanitation, and health care, but these gains are often accompanied by increasing environmental degradation that may be followed by declines in local economies and the societies they supported.

In 1999, the world's population hit 6 billion. United Nations experts predict the world will have to find resources for a population of 9 billion people in 50 years. Yet our demands on the world's natural resources are growing even faster than our numbers: since 1950, the population has more than doubled, but the global economy has quintupled. And the benefits are not equally spread; most of the economic growth has occurred in a relatively few industrialized countries.

At the same time, our settlement patterns are changing our relationship with the environment. Nearly half the world's people live in towns and cities. For many people, nature seems remote from their everyday lives. More and more people associate food with stores, rather than with their natural source. . . .

The Value of Biodiversity

Protecting biodiversity is in our self-interest. Biological resources are the pillars upon which we build civilizations. Nature's products support such diverse industries as agriculture, cosmetics, pharmaceuticals, pulp and paper, horticulture, construction and waste treatment. The loss of biodiversity threatens our food supplies, opportunities for recreation and tourism, and sources of wood, medicines and energy. It also interferes with essential ecological functions. . . .

"In-situ" conservation . . . focuses on conserving genes, species, and ecosystems in their natural surroundings.

Can we save the world's ecosystems, and with them the species we value and the other millions of species, some of which may produce the foods and medicines of tomorrow? The answer will lie in our ability to bring our demands into line with nature's ability to produce what we need and to safely absorb what we throw away.

The Convention on Biological Diversity

The Convention on Biological Diversity, as an international treaty, identifies a common problem, sets overall goals and policies and general obligations, and organizes technical and financial cooperation. However, the responsibility for achieving its goals rests largely with the countries themselves.

Private companies, landowners, fishermen, and farmers take most of the actions that affect biodiversity. Governments need to provide the critical role of leadership, particularly by setting rules that guide the use of natural resources, and by protecting biodiversity where they have direct control over the land and water. Under the Convention, governments undertake to conserve and sustainably use biodiversity. They are required to develop national biodiversity strategies and action plans, and to integrate these into broader national plans for environment and development. This is particularly important for such sectors as forestry, agriculture, fisheries, energy, transportation and urban planning. Other treaty commitments include:

- Identifying and monitoring the important components of biological diversity that need to be conserved and used sustainably.

- Establishing protected areas to conserve biological diversity while promoting environmentally sound development around these areas.

- Rehabilitating and restoring degraded ecosystems and promoting the recovery of threatened species in collaboration with local residents.

- Respecting, preserving and maintaining traditional knowledge of the sustainable use of biological diversity with the involvement of indigenous peoples and local communities.

- Preventing the introduction of, controlling, and eradicating alien species that could threaten ecosystems, habitats or species.

- Controlling the risks posed by organisms modified by biotechnology.

- Promoting public participation, particularly when it comes to assessing the environmental impacts of development projects that threaten biological diversity.

- Educating people and raising awareness about the importance of biological diversity and the need to conserve it.

- Reporting on how each country is meeting its biodiversity goals. . . .

Conservation and Sustainable Use

One of the first steps towards a successful national biodiversity strategy is to conduct surveys to find out what biodiversity exists, its value and importance, and what is endangered. On the basis of these survey results, governments can set measurable targets for conservation and sustainable use. National strategies and programmes need to be developed or adapted to meet these targets. . . .

The Convention's success depends on the combined efforts of the world's nations.

The conservation of each country's biological diversity can be achieved in various ways. "In-situ" conservation—the primary means of conservation—focuses on conserving genes, species, and ecosystems in their natural surroundings, for example, by establishing protected areas, rehabilitating degraded ecosystems, and adopting legislation to protect threatened species. "Ex-situ" conservation uses zoos, botanical gardens and gene banks to conserve species.

Promoting the sustainable use of biodiversity will be of growing importance for maintaining biodiversity in the years and decades to come. Under the Convention, the "ecosystem approach to the conservation and sustainable use of biodiversity" is being used as a framework for action, in which all the goods and services provided by the biodiversity in ecosystems are considered. The Convention is promoting activities to ensure that everyone benefits from such goods and services in an equitable way.

There are many examples of initiatives to integrate the objectives of conservation and sustainable use:

- In 1994, Uganda adopted a programme under which protected wildlife areas shared part of their tourism revenues with local people. This approach is now being used in several African countries.

- In recognition of the environmental services that forests provide to the nation, Costa Rica's 1996 Forestry Law includes provisions to compensate private landowners and forest managers who maintain or increase the area of forest within their properties.

- In different parts of the world, farmers are raising crops within mixed ecosystems. In Mexico, they are growing "shade coffee," putting coffee trees in a mixed tropical forest rather than in monoculture plantations that reduce biodiversity. These farmers then rely entirely on natural predators common to an intact ecosystem rather than on chemical pesticides.

- Tourists, attracted in large numbers by the spectacular beauty of marine and coastal diversity of the Soufrière area of St. Lucia, had a negative impact on the age-old and thriving fishing industry. In 1992, several institutions joined with fisher-folk and other groups with an interest in conservation and sustainable management of the resources and, together, established the Soufrière Marine Management Area. Within this framework, problems are dealt with on a participatory basis with the involvement of all stakeholders.

- Through weekly "farmer field schools," rice farmers in several Asian countries have developed their understanding of the functioning of the tropical rice ecosystem including the interactions between insect pests of rice, their natural enemies, fish farmed in the rice paddies, and the crop itself—to improve their crop management practices. This way they have increased their crop yields, while at the same time almost eliminating insecticide use with positive benefits in terms of environmental and human health. About 2 million farmers have benefited from this approach.

- In Tanzania, problems surrounding the sustainable use of Lake Manyara, a large freshwater lake, arose following increased usage in recent decades. The formation of the Lake Manyara Biosphere Reserve to combine both conservation of the lake and surrounding high value forests with sustainable use of the wetlands area and simple agriculture has brought together key users to set management goals. The Biosphere Reserve has fostered studies for the sustainable management of the wetlands, including monitoring the ground water and the chemistry of the escarpment water source.

- Clayoquot Sound on the western coast of Vancouver Island, Canada, encompasses forests and marine and coastal systems. The establishment of adaptive management to implement the ecosystem approach at the local level is currently under development with the involvement of indigenous communities, with a view to ensuring rational use of the forest and marine resources.

- Sian Ka'an Biosphere Reserve in Mexico has great cultural value with its 23 recorded Mayan and other archaeological sites while also being the home of some 800 people, mainly of Mayan descent. The reserve forms part of the extensive barrier reef system along the eastern coastline of Central America and includes coastal dunes, mangroves, marshes and inundated and upland forests. The inclusion of local people in its management helps maintain the balance between pure conservation and the need for sustainable use of re-sources by the local community . . .

International Action Necessary

The Convention's success depends on the combined efforts of the world's nations. The responsibility to implement the Convention lies with the individual countries and, to a large extent, compliance will depend on informed self-interest and peer pressure from other countries and from public opinion. The Convention has created a global forum—actually a series of meetings—where governments, non-governmental organizations, academics, the private sector and other interested groups or individuals share ideas and compare strategies.

Developing countries emphasized that their ability . . . to achieve global biodiversity benefits would depend on financial and technical assistance.

The Convention's ultimate authority is the Conference of the Parties (COP), consisting of all governments (and regional economic integration organizations) that have ratified the treaty. This governing body reviews progress under the Convention, identifies new priorities, and sets work plans for members. The COP can also make amendments to the Convention, create expert advisory bodies, review progress reports by member nations, and collaborate with other international organizations and agreements. . . .

Financial and Technical Support for Developing Countries

When the Convention was adopted, developing countries emphasized that their ability to take national actions to achieve global biodiversity benefits would depend on financial and technical assistance. Thus, bilateral and multilateral support for capacity building and for investing in projects and programmes is essential for enabling developing countries to meet the Convention's objectives.

Convention-related activities by developing countries are eligible for support from the financial mechanism of the Convention: the Global Environment Facility (GEF). GEF projects, supported by the United Nations Environment Programme (UNEP), the United Nations Development Programme (UNDP) and the World Bank, help forge international cooperation and finance actions to address four critical threats to the global environment: biodiversity loss, climate change, depletion of the ozone layer and degradation of international waters. By the end of 1999, the GEF had contributed nearly $1 billion for biodiversity projects in more than 120 countries. . . .

The Challenges Ahead

Economic development is essential to meeting human needs and to eliminating the poverty that affects so many people around the world. The sustainable use of nature is essential for the long-term success of development strategies. A major challenge for the 21st century will be making the conservation and sustainable use of biodiversity a compelling basis for development policies, business decisions, and consumer desires. . . .

Sadly, it often still pays to exploit the environment now by harvesting as much as possible as fast as possible.

The Convention has already accomplished a great deal on the road to sustainable development by transforming the international community's approach to biodiversity. This progress has been driven by the Convention's inherent strengths of near universal membership, a comprehensive and science-driven mandate, international financial support for national projects, world-class scientific and technological advice, and the political involvement of governments. It has brought together, for the first time, people with very different interests. It offers hope for the future by forging a new deal between governments, economic interests, environmentalists, indigenous peoples and local communities, and the concerned citizen.

However, many challenges still lie ahead. After a surge of interest in the wake of the Rio Summit, many observers are disappointed by the slow progress towards sustainable development during the 1990s. Attention to environmental problems was distracted by a series of economic crises, budget deficits, and local and regional conflicts. Despite the promise of Rio, economic growth without adequate environmental safeguards is still the rule rather than the exception. . . .

The Convention on Biological Diversity and its underlying concepts can be difficult to communicate to politicians and to the general public. Nearly a decade after the Convention first acknowledged the lack of information and knowledge regarding biological diversity, it remains an issue that few people understand. There is little public discussion of how to make sustainable use of biodiversity part of economic development. The greatest crunch in sustainable development decisions is the short- versus the long-term time frame. Sadly, it often still pays to exploit the environment now by harvesting as much as possible as fast as possible because economic rules do little to protect long-term interests.

Truly sustainable development requires countries to redefine their policies on land use, food, water, energy, employment, development, conservation, economics, and trade. Biodiversity protection and sustainable use requires the participation of ministries responsible for such areas as agriculture, forestry, fisheries, energy, tourism, trade and finance.

The challenge facing governments, businesses, and citizens is to forge transition strategies leading to long-term sustainable development. It means negotiating trade-offs even as people are clamoring for more land and businesses are pressing for concessions to expand their harvests. The longer we wait, the fewer options we will have.

The Rainforests Can Be Saved with Sustainable Logging and Agriculture

The Economist

The Economist is a British news magazine that covers world business, current affairs, finance, science, and technology matters.

Use it or lose it. The mantra is applied as much to the rainforest and the rest of the natural world as to the artificial. But exploitation does not have to involve destruction. And there are powerful reasons for seeking to avoid the destruction of wilderness and the concomitant extinction of species.

The Value of Biodiversity

The strongest argument for conserving biodiversity is to protect the "ecosystems" on which humanity itself depends. Diversified ecosystems protect watersheds, local rainfall, food supply and soil. The Amazon ecosystem is so vast that it creates its own climate. Most rainfall is recycled, and the forest affects light reflection, cloud formation, regional rainfall and temperature. Most important, the rainforest is also a bulwark against global warming. You cannot chop it down or burn it without running large climatic risks.

From the American mid-west to Bangladesh to Mozambique, the costs of deforestation are now being felt in the form of altered climates, droughts, flash floods, landslides and soil erosion. The result can be human and economic suffering on a grand scale. Once created, such suffering is not easy to cure. In the long run, reforestation may be the only answer, but plantations do not function as well as a diversified forest that is the product of several thousand years of evolution.

The rate at which species are being lost is so high that ... [it may be likened] to earlier mass extinctions such as the one that killed the dinosaurs.

Ten years ago, few people appreciated the effect of wide biodiversity on ecosystems. But it is not hard to grasp the case for keeping more species. Having more species in an ecosystem gives it more stability, allows it to retain more nutrients and makes it more productive. There is an analogy with the diversification gains to be had from spreading an investment portfolio. Species, like shares, differ from one another, and they respond differently to external events. The more species, therefore, the less volatile and unstable the ecosystem. Moreover, different species specialise in particular niches that make the best use of different resources and of changes in, say, soil acidity and temperature.

Some ecologists reckon that the rate at which species are being lost is so high that, if it continues, palaeontologists of the future will look at the fossil record now being laid down and liken it to earlier mass extinctions such as the one that killed the dinosaurs. Those previous extinctions are thought to have been triggered by external shocks such as an asteroid impact or a huge volcanic eruption. But how much of each previous extinction—in which around 95% of all species were lost—was caused directly by the shock, and how much by a subsequent unravelling of the ecosystem due to the loss of specific habitats and species, remains unknown. What seems certain is that finding out by repeating the experiment will be a risky and unpleasant experience: people, for all their artificial cushions, are part of the ecosystem too.

There is also opportunity cost to consider: the things extinction could make harder. All crops, garden plants and domestic animals have wild ancestors. Corn, rice and wheat alone provide 60% of the human food supply. Their continued viability depends on the maintenance of the genetic diversity of their ancestors, which alone makes possible the breeding of new strains that are resistant to evolving diseases and pests.

Fortunately, the world's growing understanding of the value of biodiversity is coming at the same time as the discovery of ways to make it pay without destroying it.

For many rich-world conservationists the value of preserving biodiversity is more a matter of sentiment and aesthetics than of pragmatism. People do not burn Picassos or cathedrals, so why should they burn the Amazon rainforest? There is nothing wrong with this question—economic arguments sometimes come second to ethical or aesthetic ones—but it does need to be recognised that all such "external public goods" have to be paid for, even if the cost comes only in benefits forgone.

Reasons for Optimism

Fortunately, the world's growing understanding of the value of biodiversity is coming at the same time as the discovery of ways to make it pay without destroying it. The new approach is, with fits and starts, being adopted in Brazil. This has included the removal of subsidies and of perverse tax incentives that encouraged otherwise uneconomic forest destruction. It also identifies the forest as a sustainable resource that can yield a crop rather than being a one-off "mine" for timber that, when cleared, is largely unsuitable for farming. New systems of reduced-impact logging appear to be just as feasible as conventional reckless logging, while being far less damaging.

The environmental sensibilities of western consumers are also being co-opted by selling, at a premium, forest products from areas that can be certified as following good management practices.

Another encouraging change arises because Brazil, though not exactly a rich country, is no longer a poor one. A conservationist movement is stirring among the new middle classes, and beginning to win some battles. One gram of patriotic pressure is often worth a tonne of well-meaning foreign meddling.

Ultimately, the new conservation boils down to a more sophisticated approach by private firms—from loggers to fruit distributors—to working out how a stretch of forest can be made into a long-term source of profitable business. It seems that Brazil is groping for ways of reconciling the interests of people who live in the forest (including those living in towns in the forest), those who live off the forest, those who depend on the forest for other services such as hydropower—and those who simply want to keep the forest as it is.

A report this week [of May 12, 2001] from the World Conservation Union and a Washington-based organisation, Future Harvest, says that biodiversity hotspots are often being threatened by the demands of agriculture. But the report also points to an emerging set of strategies it calls "ecoagriculture", which show how to minimise conflicts between the demands of agriculture and those of biodiversity. Out of the woods, in short, come some new grounds for optimism. If Brazil can also deal with the problem of lawlessness and corruption, it can easily improve on the abysmal record of largely deforested first-world countries (from which Brazil is understandably unwilling to take hypocritical lectures). With luck, Brazil might even inspire other tropical countries to follow suit.

Following Natural Design Principles Can Protect Biodiversity

William McDonough

William McDonough is an architect, an innovator in sustainable design, and the author, with Michael Braungart, of the book Cradle to Cradle: Remaking the Way We Make Things.

When architectural historian Vincent Scully gave a eulogy for the great architect Louis Kahn, he described a day when both were crossing Red Square, whereupon Scully excitedly turned to Kahn and said, "Isn't it wonderful the way the domes of St. Basil's Cathedral reach up into the sky?" Kahn looked up and down thoughtfully for a moment and said, "Isn't it beautiful the way they come down to the ground?"

If we understand that design leads to the manifestation of human intention, and if what we make with our hands is to be sacred and honor the earth that gives us life, then the things we make must not only rise from the ground but return to it, soil to soil, water to water, so everything that is received from the earth can be freely given back without causing harm to any living system. This is ecology. This is good design.

The Natural World As a Model for Human Designs

We can use certain fundamental laws inherent to the natural world as models and mentors for human designs. Ecology comes from the Greek roots oikos and logos, "household" and "logical discourse." Thus it is appropriate, if not imperative,

William McDonough, "Ecology, Ethics, and the Making of Things: A World-Renowned Architect Argues that Following the Law of Nature Can Make Human Industry Safe and Healthful," *Sojourners*, vol. 34, iss. 5, May 2005, p. 36, 38. Copyright © 2005 *Sojourners*. Reproduced with permission from the author.

for architects to discourse about the logic of our earth household. To do so, we must first look at our planet and the very processes by which it manifests life, because therein lie the logical principles with which we must work. And we must also consider economy in the true sense of the word. Using the Greek words oikos and nomos, we speak of natural law and how we measure and manage the relationships within this household, working with the principles our discourse has revealed to us.

The one thing allowing nature to continually cycle itself through life is energy ... in the form of perpetual solar income.

There are three defining characteristics that we can learn from natural design. The first is that all materials given to us by nature are constantly returned to the earth without even the concept of waste as we understand it. Everything is cycled constantly with all waste equaling food for other living systems.

The second characteristic is that the one thing allowing nature to continually cycle itself through life is energy, and this energy comes from outside the system in the form of perpetual solar income. Not only does nature operate on "current income," it does not mine or extract energy from the past, it does not use its capital reserves, and it does not borrow from the future.

Finally, the characteristic that sustains this complex and efficient system of metabolism and creation is biodiversity. What prevents living systems from running down and veering into chaos is a miraculously intricate and symbiotic relationship between millions of organisms, no two of which are alike.

As a designer of buildings, things, and systems, I ask myself how to apply these three characteristics of living systems to my work. How do I employ the concept of waste equals food, of current solar income, of protecting biodiversity in design?

Consumables, Durables, and Unmarketables

My colleague Michael Braungart, an ecological chemist from Hamburg, Germany, has pointed out that we should remove the word "waste" from our vocabulary and start using the word "product" instead, because if waste is going to equal food, it must also be a product. Braungart suggests we think about three distinct product types:

First, there are consumables. We should be producing more of them. These are products that when eaten or used, or thrown away, literally turn back into dirt and therefore are food for other living organisms. Consumables should not be placed in landfills but put on the ground so that they restore the life, health, and fertility of the soil. This means shampoo bottles made of beets that are biodegradable in your compost pile and carpets that break down into CO_2 and water.

When we . . . embrace the intention of creating only safe, healthful, restorative things, the purview of design shifts radically.

Second are products of service, also known as durables, such as cars and television sets. They are called products of service because what people want is the service the product provides—food, entertainment, or transportation. To eliminate the concept of waste, products of service would not be sold but licensed to the end-user. Customers may use them as long as they wish, even sell the license to someone else, but when the end-user is finished with, say, a television, it goes back to Sony, Zenith, or Philips. It is "food" for their system, but not for natural systems.

The third type of product is called "unmarketables." Why would anyone produce a product that no one would buy? Welcome to the world of nuclear waste, dioxins, and chromium-tanned leather. We are essentially making products or subcomponents of products that no one should buy or, in many cases, do not realize they are buying.

When we take seriously the idea that the very concept of waste can be eliminated, when we stop trying to be "less bad" by merely limiting the destructive effects of architecture and industry and instead embrace the intention of creating only safe, healthful, restorative things, the purview of design shifts radically.

Honoring the Sacred

I remember when we were hired to design the office for an environmental group. The director said at the end of contract negotiations, "By the way, if anybody in our office gets sick from indoor air quality, we're going to sue you." After wondering if we should even take the job, we decided to go ahead, that it was our job to find the materials that wouldn't make people sick when placed inside a building. And what we found is that those materials weren't there. We had to work with manufacturers to find out what was in their products, and we discovered that the entire system of building construction is essentially toxic. We are still working on the materials side.

For a New York men's clothing store, we arranged for the planting of 1,000 oak trees to replace the two English oaks used to panel the store. We were inspired by a famous story told by Gregory Bateson about New College in Oxford, England. It went something like this. They had a main hall built in the early 1600s with beams 40 feet long and 2 feet thick. A committee was formed to try to find replacement trees because the beams were suffering from dry rot. If you keep in mind that veneer from an English oak can be worth $7 a square foot, the total replacement cost for the oaks was prohibitively expensive. And they didn't have straight 40-foot English oaks from mature forests with which to replace the beams.

We must come to peace with and accept our place in the natural world.

A young faculty member joined the committee and said, "Why don't we ask the college forester if some of the lands that have been given to Oxford might have enough trees to call upon?" And when they brought in the forester, he said, "We've been wondering when you would ask this question. When the present building was constructed 350 years ago, the architects specified that a grove of trees be planted and maintained to replace the beams in the ceiling when they would suffer from dry rot." Bateson's remark was, "That's the way to run a culture." Our question and hope is, "Did they replant them?"

We have to recognize that every event and manifestation of nature is "design," that to live within the laws of nature means to express our human intention as an interdependent species, aware and grateful that we are at the mercy of sacred forces larger than ourselves, and that we obey these laws in order to honor the sacred in each other and in all things. We must come to peace with and accept our place in the natural world.

Smarter Management of the Oceans Would Allow Sea Life to Rebound

Ben Carmichael

Ben Carmichael is a writer and a frequent contributor to OnEarth, an environmental magazine published by the National Resources Defense Council, an environmental action organization.

Fish populations are in free fall; the food supply of millions of people around the world is in jeopardy. Seabed-scouring trawlers and reckless overharvesting are devastating vast webs of ocean life, and the species we eat aren't the only ones to suffer. From majestic sea turtles to wondrous deepwater organisms with their startlingly unique arrays of DNA, the underwater realm is in peril.

The Status of Marine Biodiversity

In reaction to the rapid loss of marine biodiversity, an international team of scientists and economists led by the biologist Boris Worm at Dalhousie University in Halifax, Nova Scotia, published a study in the November 3, 2006, issue of the journal *Science* in which they analyzed more than 50 years' worth of fisheries and ecological monitoring data. All told, the study examined 83 percent of the world catch during that time period to create a comprehensive picture of what the decline in marine biodiversity means for humans. By midcentury, the team concluded, many fish and shellfish species could collapse, their commercial catches reduced to a mere tenth of their historical highs. But the study also offered some promis-

Ben Carmichael, "Charting a New Course to Save Our Seas: A Landmark Study Offers an Urgent Directive to Revive the Oceans," *OnEarth*, vol. 29, iss. 1, spring 2007, pp. 42–43. Copyright © 2007 Natural Resources Defense Council. Reproduced by permission.

ing news: It's not too late. The trend is reversible; ecosystems with the greatest biodiversity appear more able to heal themselves than those with fewer distinct species. With smarter, more forward-looking management, ocean life could rebound.

"This study helps answer one of the central questions in the field of ecology, which is: 'What is the role of biodiversity?'" says Lisa Suatoni, an evolutionary biologist and NRDC [National Resource Defense Council] science fellow. "The answer, it seems, is that biodiversity translates into resilience."

Like a healthy immune system, diversity gives oceans the strength to recover from injury, whether caused by overfishing, pollution, or destruction of habitat by trawling. Enabling the seas to heal in this way requires adopting the very principles that NRDC's oceans program works to promote: Create protected marine areas similar to wildlife preserves on land, stop overfishing, and make management decisions that take into account all of the interconnected species within an ecosystem. Species near the top of the food chain—the ones we eat, such as cod and swordfish—could then flourish.

Efforts to Protect the Oceans

It is not only scientists who are realizing the wisdom of such an approach. Last fall [2006], California proposed protections for a network of 29 marine areas covering more than 200 square miles of state waters, four times the area of San Francisco. The goal is to create safe havens where a wide range of marine life can coexist unfettered by human activity, thereby boosting biodiversity and replenishing depleted populations. NRDC scientists and policy experts played an instrumental role in gathering support for the state's Marine Life Protection Act, passed in 1999, which paved the way for the new designations; they are now helping to implement the law.

Other states are moving to rehabilitate their waters as well. New York, for example, has passed a law that will encourage the application of more enlightened, interdisciplinary management practices to protect marine species and habitats, from wetland nurseries to deepwater environments. NRDC worked with state agencies and legislators to pass the law and will continue to work with agency officials to promote its implementation.

On a national level, the recent reauthorization of the landmark Magnuson-Stevens Fishery Conservation and Management Act should prove a boon to oceans beyond coastal states' offshore boundaries. The law is named in part for Senator Ted Stevens, Republican of Alaska, who has proven a consistent supporter of the common-sense idea that the surest way to maintain profitable commercial fisheries, in his home state and elsewhere, is to prevent overfishing. The reauthorization bill, signed into law on January 12, strengthens the existing law, passed in 1976, by setting a firm deadline for ending overfishing and requiring the use of current scientific data in establishing quotas. Working closely with key Senate and House staff members, NRDC brought its legal, scientific, and economic expertise to the debate and played a leading role in the reauthorization process.

"This is about protecting some of our most magnificent places and safeguarding the well-being of millions of people who rely on them," says Karen Garrison, an NRDC oceans policy expert. "The underwater world is as precious, as wild and beautiful—and as necessary—as the wilderness of Yosemite. But we are playing catch-up in the oceans."

Reducing the Human Population While Expanding Conservation Practices Provides the Best Chances for Reversing Biodiversity Loss

Tatiana Siegel

Tatiana Siegel is a writer at the Environmental Policy Center in San Francisco whose criticism has also appeared in the San Francisco Chronicle *and the* Providence Journal.

As the Earth's population surges toward the 7 billion mark, the following twist on an old maxim perhaps best applies: A single birth is a joyous occasion. A billion births is a tragedy. . . . When the planet's human head count topped the 6 billion threshold in 1999, few pundits seemed to grasp the catastrophic ecological implications. Rush Limbaugh weighed in with frequent assurances that the entire global population could fit comfortably in the state of Texas. But as the planet endures an alarming net gain of more than 73 million a year, or some 200,000 people a day, it would be naive to think that this explosion can occur without grave environmental repercussions.

Population Growth and Biodiversity

Until now, there has been a dearth of literature linking human population growth and biodiversity loss. However, Jeffrey K. McKee's stunning, albeit flawed, new book *Sparing Nature* pinpoints the precise moment (in geological terms) when our early ancestors' success resulted in the death of neighboring species—roughly 1.8 million years ago, the arrival of Homo erectus. Around that time, African mammals began to disappear at an unparalleled pace. But the biodiversity crisis really accelerated, McKee establishes, at the onset of the agriculture age, some 10,000 years ago, when humans enjoyed unprecedented growth. The book then takes the cause-effect model one step further and assesses what the mass decline of species diversification means for the continuity of the human race.

McKee, an anthropology professor at Ohio State University and co-author of *The Riddled Chain: Chance, Coincidence, and Chaos in Human Evolution*, offers several theses in *Sparing Nature*. He argues that preserving biodiversity is essential to the health of the planet, and consequently the long-term survival of the human species. On this point, he offers incontrovertible evidence. Mining the fossil record, McKee demonstrates that it is no coincidence that our impressive proliferation also corresponds with what many scientists believe is the planet's sixth major period of mass extinction. And as history reveals, mass extinctions don't bode well for the top of the food chain (just ask the victims of Mass Extinction No. 5—the dinosaurs).

Humans, McKee notes, have a long and troubling history of muscling out other species through a myriad of practices, including agriculture, irrigation, habitat destruction, pollution, the introduction of invasive species and our latest contribution—the dramatic and irresponsible overproduction of greenhouse gases. While tropical rainforests are cleared in order to make room for farms, McKee ruefully observes, the constant felling has generated a mere 13 percent of the world's cropland, yet it has spelled disaster for disproportionately high numbers of flora and fauna. For example, of the known plant species worldwide, at least one in eight is threatened or hovers near the brink of extinction. To date, human activity has put 40-50 percent of the Earth's available land out of commission to a vast number of species, which are critical to eco-stability.

Furthermore, these lands have now been rendered worthless even to humans because of overfarming and excessive development.

Not all humans leave a similar footprint on the ecological landscape.

Some may ask, so what if we lose a minor species here or there in the march of progress? To many, the loss of Northern California's endangered tiger salamander (threatened by sprawl) would represent a far less significant loss than the annihilation of the mighty Bengal tiger (the public tends to respond more strongly to the large, majestic threatened animals). But McKee evinces that an absence, either large or small, in nature's master blueprint has a ripple effect. "What is lost with one type of animal are the others that depend on it. What is lost is an ecosystem."

With an elegant and earnest writing style more common among nature writers than academics, McKee tallies the value of a balanced ecosystem, explaining, "These complex systems took millions of years to evolve, and the resulting web of life is not easily unwoven. The extinction of one species may have dire consequences for its coevolutionary partners. Thus, in today's highly evolved world, it takes biodiversity to sustain biodiversity." It's easy to spot other areas of life where varied components help complex entities survive and thrive, as diversity is considered good for college campuses, 401(k) portfolios and a healthy diet. Similarly, *Sparing Nature* confirms that biodiversity is integral to a healthy and robust planet, serving critical functions in everything from climate management to erosion control.

Affluent Lifestyles

Despite its sobering analysis, *Sparing Nature* is perhaps a bit too damning in one of its main points: "The impact of our large population would be great even if we were to behave differently." McKee follows up by stating that our mere presence—regardless of whether we recycle, drive a hybrid, support organic farming or eschew McDonald's—will always limit or reduce biodiversity. In short, our behavioral choices have less impact than our sheer numbers. But this contention seems to fly in the face of logic. After all, not all humans leave a similar footprint on the ecological landscape. The United States, for example, is the most prolific global polluter, and thus habitat destroyer, in many categories, particularly the generation of greenhouse-gas emissions. Yet our population is dwarfed by both China's and India's. Contrary to McKee's line of reasoning, a two-child family living in a 12,000-square-foot Westchester County home, which is heated, air-conditioned, landscaped and redecorated every two years with furniture made from Indonesian rainforest wood is having a greater impact on nature's ability to function unimpeded than a family of eight living under one roof in a Mexican village.

In fact, a study published in a January issue of the journal *Nature* found that an increase in the number of homes sheltering fewer people is more damaging to the environment than simple population growth. This trend—in which a nuclear family of four lives in a separate home rather than with the traditional extended family—is uniquely congruous with Western prosperity. The study notes that the rise in the number of dwellings with fewer occupants leads to a greater exploitation of natural resources such as land, energy, wood and water, and that this amplified use of scarce reserves is endangering species diversification.

Affluence seems to be a more overriding variable than raw numbers [of people].

McKee does make a convincing argument about the greater number of mouths to feed. At first glance, his contention holds up, as food is perhaps mankind's common denominator. Everyone needs sustenance, and man's taming of the land in the quest for food has dealt the greatest blow to biodiversity. But not all mouths are equally demanding. As Lester Brown, one of the world's most influential environmental thinkers, noted in his book *Who Will Feed China?* if the Chinese diet mirrored the Japanese diet, all the world's fish stocks would be depleted. Once again, affluence seems to be a more overriding variable than raw numbers.

The California Example

As one of the regions of the country experiencing unprecedented population pressures, California offers a unique glimpse into how human behavior shapes the landscape in a more significant way than the sum of all people. Over the next twenty years, the Golden State will add 11.3 million new residents, and the ensuing land development will undoubtedly encroach on fragile habitat. Because the growth is almost entirely due to immigration, the newcomers and their offspring tend to be blamed for the state's ecological woes. But even if California closed its borders to all future immigration, it wouldn't solve any of the most vexing environmental problems, particularly the shrinking water supply. Consider that up to three-quarters of the state's urban water use goes to landscaping—an activity more frequently associated with the wealthy and middle class than the newly arrived.

Most land-use experts concur that population growth isn't the primary cause of environmental degradation. Rather, historic land-use patterns, which have resulted in a car-dependent culture, continue to wreak havoc on the natural world. And while it undercuts their own best interests, Californians hate density (a term often erroneously confused with crowding). Paris is one of the most densely populated cities in the world, yet it is heralded as one of the most livable. Unfortunately, most Californians think "livable" equals a single-family home with a yard, even if it entails a three-hour daily commute and horrible air quality. That's why the state has become synonymous with sprawl. And according to the National Wildlife Federation, sprawl is the leading cause of species imperilment in California, outranking all other factors. While countless plants, insects, reptiles, birds and animals indigenous to California survived the Ice Age, they may be defenseless against the Age of the Subdivision.

A 2001 Sierra Club report that examined nationwide land-use patterns reached similar conclusions. The report found that population growth accounts for only 31 percent of America's land consumption. Much of the rest can be blamed on ill-conceived land-use planning and government subsidies that encourage sprawl. According to Cornell University professor Rolf Pendall, "It is clear that population increases are not the only contributor to sprawl. Increasing population growth is most problematic when it happens in regions with poor land-use decision-making."

The problem with McKee's numbers-trump-behavior argument is that it unintentionally absolves societies—like the United States—that largely keep their population growth in check. However, when the United States withdrew from the Kyoto Protocol negotiations in 2001, it committed to a path of habitat destruction that outweighs any progress it can make in reducing its population.

Nevertheless, population growth does pose a grave risk to our global environment. As we add enough new people to the planet every thirty-eight days to populate a new New York City, McKee's call to stem and perhaps even reduce our numbers is undoubtedly warranted. The Bush Administration's withdrawal last July of the $34 million it had promised to support the UN Population Fund wasted an opportunity to spread the message of responsible family planning. While the move understandably drew criticism from women's rights advocates, few discussed the decision's environmental fallout. As

McKee dejectedly notes, "It comes down to this question: do we want fewer children who have more to appreciate, or more children who have less to appreciate?" And don't count on a mighty plague to restore the Earth's equilibrium. McKee maintains that "the rise of disease probably will not be enough to seriously stem our persistent population growth—it will just be enough to make us miserable."

In the absence of viable population-reduction prescriptions, conservation efforts remain our greatest chance for reversing global cataclysm.

Unfortunately, McKee, much like mankind, waits until the final chapter to discuss possible solutions. And even then, his suggestions are vague. *Sparing Nature* calls for population-growth abatement and improved family planning. But the only proposal he offers is to foster a global conscientiousness through education about the perils of overpopulation. It's a noble-sounding gesture, but is it realistic? McKee briefly cites one successful model: The Iranian government offered free vasectomies for married men, distributed contraceptives and slashed its population growth in half. It's a program that should definitely be studied and perhaps replicated.

While McKee believes that eco-friendly lifestyle choices are well-meaning, he thinks it would be more beneficial, and perhaps easier, simply to cease population growth worldwide. But in the absence of viable population-reduction prescriptions, conservation efforts remain our greatest chance for reversing global cataclysm.

Stabilizing the Human Population by Empowering Women Can Help Protect Biodiversity

Mia MacDonald and Danielle Nierenberg

Mia MacDonald is a senior fellow and Danielle Nierenberg is a senior researcher at the Worldwatch Institute, an independent research organization that works to promote an environmentally sustainable and socially just society. This article is adapted from "Linking Population, Women and Biodiversity," part of "State of the World 2003," a report published by Worldwatch.

In and around the Kiunga National Marine Reserve on Kenya's [an African nation] northern coast, basic services such as running water, electricity and health care are hard to come by. Post-primary education, especially for girls, is scarce. Pushed by poverty and the decline of marine ecosystems further down the coast, local residents and migrants are intensifying their use of resources. Fish, crustaceans, ocean-dwelling coral and turtles are showing signs of stress.

In Kiunga, as in several other priority biodiversity conservation regions where girls rarely complete high school, fertility rates remain high and women's roles in resource use and protection are often ignored, the World Wildlife Fund is supporting a small number of girls' scholarships. These are paired with environmental education, including in-school activities and a week-long conservation camp.

One result is a change in attitude. Swabra, 16, a scholarship recipient, has become an advocate of marine conservation. "In our area, people were eating turtles," she says. "Now I

Mia MacDonald and Danielle Nierenberg, "A Clear Connection: Empowering Women Results in Smaller Populations that Preserve Biodiversity," *E*, vol. 14, iss. 3, May–June 2003, pp. 18, 20–21. Copyright © 2003. Reproduced with permission from *E/The Environmental Magazine*.

know the importance of conserving them. I've educated the whole community by telling them it is not good to eat turtles." At weekly community meetings, teachers urge parents to send girls to school and keep them there.

Population, Biodiversity, and Gender

World population is now [as of 2003] more than 6.2 billion and growing by 77 million a year, equivalent to the combined 2001 populations of Mozambique, Paraguay, Poland, Portugal and Singapore. The rate of growth is slowing, however: Globally, women now have about half as many children as their mothers did (an average of just under three children each). Still, the United Nations suggests that by 2050 about 8.9 billion people will be sharing the planet—nearly 50 percent more than today. The numbers are still shockingly high, but lower than previous estimates. New UN projections foresee about 400 million fewer people by 2050 than expected just two years ago, the result of a heavier toll of AIDS deaths combined with dropping fertility rates.

Where women are free to determine when and whether they will have children, fertility rates fall.

In the 1990s, professionals both in and out of government began to see and act on the connections between population, biodiversity and gender, often taking their cues from agreements reached at UN [United Nations] conferences in Rio, Cairo and Beijing. These usually small initiatives (which include the WWF scholarship program) provide fertile ground for nurturing larger-scale, more robust actions.

The potential impacts are considerable. "Many biodiversity-rich areas are among the last places on Earth for average fertility to fall from its historic high levels," observes Robert Engelman of Population Action International, "probably because such places tend to be farthest from the reach of cities, services and the electronic media. But these also are often the places where fertility is falling fastest, precisely because the modern world is just reaching them, and traditional ideas of childbearing and women's roles are changing rapidly."

The poorest, least-developed countries tend to combine rapid population growth, low status for women and rich biodiversity. The global community now accepts that where women are free to determine when and whether they will have children, fertility rates fall. Researchers have also shown repeatedly that the more education a woman receives, the fewer children she has and the healthier and better educated those children are. Other studies suggest that if women have the right and ability to manage childbearing, they can manage other areas of their life more effectively, too, including available resources.

While women are gaining power to determine the direction of their lives, large gaps remain. Sixty percent of the world's hundred million children not attending primary school are girls. Two-thirds of the world's illiterate people are women, and at least 350 million women lack access to a full range of contraceptive services.

Throughout the developing world, gender plays a strong role in how resources are used, controlled and developed and in how people respond to environmental challenges. Women rely heavily on natural resources in their daily lives—everything from firewood for cooking to fibers for making clothes and a variety of plants for medicine. Yet by some estimates, women hold title to less than two percent of the world's private land. "Since rights to natural resources are so heavily biased against women," reasons Agnes Quisumbing of the International Food Policy Research Institute, "equalizing these rights will lead to more efficient and equitable resource use."

Lorena Aguilar, senior gender advisor at the International Union for Conservation of Nature and Natural Resources (IUCN), sees gender equity as the "unavoidable current" determining the impact of conservation policies and programs. Awareness of this is lacking in the upper reaches of government, but community programs that address these links have been launched, often through conservation and development agencies.

In the state of Chiapas, Mexico, Conservation International has begun working with a family planning group, Mexfam, and the Mexican Social Security Institute to expand access to reproductive health care, including family planning, and to halt the clearing of forests in and around the Montes Azules Biosphere Reserve. In the mountainous provinces of central Ecuador, World Neighbors, a development organization, has joined with the locally based Center for Medical Guidance and Family Planning to deliver reproductive health care and to promote improvements in local management of natural resources to more than 4,000 families.

Advancing gender equity . . . may be one of the best ways of saving the environment.

And in Tanzania, in response to serious deforestation outside the borders of the Gombe National Park, the Jane Goodall Institute established the Lake Tanganyika Catchment Reforestation and Education (TACARE) program in 1994. TACARE now works in 30 villages on soil erosion and deforestation issues, combining them with economic development.

Programs like this come none too soon. As Nobel Prize-winning economist Amartya Sen points out, "The population problem is integrally linked with justice for women in particular. Advancing gender equity, through reversing the various social and economic handicaps that make women voiceless and powerless, may also be one of the best ways of saving the environment, working against global warming and countering the dangers of overcrowding and other adversities associated with population pressure. The voice of women is critically important for the world's future—not just for women's future."

Organizations to Contact

The editors have compiled the following list of organizations concerned with the issues debated in this book. The descriptions are derived from materials provided by the organizations. All have publications or information available for interested readers. The list was compiled on the date of publication of the present volume; the information provided here may change. Readers need to remember that many organizations take several weeks or longer to respond to inquiries.

Biodiversity Project
214 N. Henry St., Suite 201, Madison, WI   53703
(608) 250-9876 • Fax: (608) 257-3513
E-mail: project@biodiverse.org
Web site: www.biodiversityproject.org

The Biodiversity Project was founded in 1995 by a group of grantmakers, scientists, and advocates. Its mission is to make people aware of the importance of biodiversity and, through public education and communications programs, empower them to take actions to protect nature. The group's Web site sells numerous publications.

Biodiversity Support Program
c/o World Wildlife Fund, 1250 24th Street, NW
Washington, D.C.   20037
(207) 293-4800 • Fax: (800) 858-4844
Web site: www.bsponline.org

The Biodiversity Support Program, a project of the World Wildlife Fund, The Nature Conservancy, and World Resources Institute, promotes conservation of the world's biological diversity by integrating conservation with social and economic development, research and analysis, and information exchange and outreach. The site contains a link to a list of publications on biodiversity topics.

Center for Biodiversity and Conservation
American Museum of Natural History
Central Park West at 79th St., New York, NY   10024
(212) 769-5742 • Fax: (212) 769-5292
E-mail: biodiversity@amnh.org
Web site: http://research.amnh.org/biodiversity

The Center for Biodiversity and Conservation was created by
the American Museum of Natural History to integrate scientific research, education, and outreach in order to encourage
people to participate in the conservation of biodiversity. The
Center publishes papers, educational materials, field reports,
and brochures on conservation issues.

Ecological Society of America (ESA)
2010 Massachusetts Ave., N.W., Suite 400
Washington, D.C.   20036-1023
(202) 833-8773 • Fax: (202) 833-8775
E-mail: esahq@esa.org
Web site: www.esa.org

The Ecological Society of America (ESA) is a nonpartisan,
nonprofit organization of scientists founded in 1915 to improve communication among ecologists, raise the public's
awareness about ecology, increase the resources available for
the conduct of ecological science, and promote the use of ecological science in environmental decision making. The ESA
Web site provides links to policy papers, science resources,
and news about various environmental issues, including biodiversity.

Food and Agriculture Organization of the United Nations (FAO): Biodiversity
Viale delle Terme di Caracalla, Rome   00100
   Italy
(+39) 06 57051 • Fax: (+39) 06 570 53152
Email: FAO-HQ@fao.org
Web site: www.fao.org/biodiversity

The Food and Agriculture Organization of the United Nations (FAO) leads international efforts to defeat hunger. It provides information, helps developing countries modernize, and acts as a neutral forum in which all nations meet as equals to negotiate agreements and debate policy. Its Web site on biodiversity explores the connection between biodiversity and food security issues.

International Union for the Conservation of Nature and Natural Resources (ICUN)
Rue Mauverney 28, Gland
  1196
  Switzerland
(+41) (22) 999-0000 • Fax: (+41) (22) 999-0002
Web site: www.iucn.org

The International Union for the Conservation of Nature and Natural Resources (ICUN), also often called the World Conservation Union, is a global conservation network of countries, government agencies, non-governmental organizations (NGOs), scientists, and experts. The ICUN seeks to encourage the conservation of nature and to ensure that natural resources are used equitably and in ecologically sustainable ways. The ICUN Web site contains a wealth of information about biodiversity, including a list of over 3,000 publications.

National Audubon Society (NAS)
700 Broadway, New York, NY 10003
(212) 979-3000 • Fax: (212) 979-3188
E-mail: education@audubon.org
Web site: www.audubon.org

The National Audubon Society (NAS) works to conserve and restore natural ecosystems, focusing on birds, other wildlife, and their habitats for the benefit of humanity and the earth's biological diversity. It maintains a national network of community-based nature centers and chapters and conducts scientific, educational, and advocacy programs. The NAS Web site contains information on a range of issues related to biodiversity.

National Council for Science and the Environment (NCSE)
1707 H Street N.W., Suite 200
Washington, D.C.   20006-3918
(202) 530-5810 • Fax: (202) 628-4311
E-mail: info@NCSEonline.org
Web site: www.cnie.org

The National Council for Science and the Environment (NCSE) is a nonprofit organization dedicated to improving the scientific basis for environmental decision making. NCSE conducts a number of environmental education programs, accessible on its Web site, that provide information about various environmental issues, including biodiversity.

North American Biodiversity Information Network (NABIN)
Commission for Environmental Cooperation
393, rue St-Jacques Ouest, Bureau 200
Montréal, Québec
  H2Y 1N9
  Canada
(514) 350-4300 • Fax: (514) 350-4314
E-mail: info@cec.org
Web site: www.cec.org

The North American Biodiversity Information Network (NABIN) is a network of people and institutions involved in biodiversity work that seeks to bring together information sources to support decision making in the protection and conservation of biological diversity in North America. The Web site contains a list of useful publications on biodiversity topics.

The Nature Conservancy (TNC)
1815 N. Lynn Street, Arlington, VA   22209
(703) 841-5300 • Fax: (703) 841-1283
E-mail: tncmail@aol.com
Web site: www.tnc.org

The Nature Conservancy (TNC) is a leading conservation organization that works to protect ecologically important lands and waters around the globe. Its mission is to preserve the plants, animals, and natural communities that make up the Earth's biodiversity. TNC publishes *Nature Conservancy* magazine, and its Web site contains numerous articles and publications on biodiversity issues.

Seed Savers Exchange
3094 North Winn Road, Decorah, IA   52101
(563) 382-5990 • Fax: (563) 382-5872
E-mail: steph@seedsavers.org
Web site: www.seedsavers.org

This nonprofit organization is dedicated to preserving and sharing heirloom seed varieties. Its site includes information about heirloom plant varieties and an extensive catalog of heirloom seeds. The group distributes books for children, cookbooks, and gardening books and is a source for the purchase of heirloom seeds.

**World Conservation Monitoring Centre,
United Nations Environment Programme**
219 Huntingdon Road, Cambridge
  CB3 0DL
  United Kingdom
(+44) 1223-277314 • Fax: (+44) 1223-277136
E-mail: info@unep-wcmc.org
Web site: www.unep-wcmc.org

The World Conservation Monitoring Centre is a collaboration between the United Nations Environment Programme, an intergovernmental organization, and WCMC 2000, a UK-based charity. It promotes biodiversity and provides authoritative biodiversity information to decision makers. The Centre's Web site contains a number of publications on biodiversity and related topics.

Bibliography

Books

Andrew Beattie, Paul R. Ehrlich, and Christine Turnbull
Wild Solutions: How Biodiversity Is Money in the Bank, New Haven, CT: Yale University Press, 2004.

Kevin J. Gaston and John I. Spicer
Biodiversity: An Introduction, Malden, MA: Blackwell, 2004.

Brian Groombridge and Martin D. Jenkins
World Atlas of Biodiversity: Earth's Living Resources in the 21st Century, Berkeley: University of California Press, 2002.

Stephen J. G. Hall and Giuseppe Bertola
Livestock Biodiversity: Genetic Resources for the Farming of the Future, Malden, MA: Blackwell, 2004.

Gene S. Helfman
Fish Conservation: A Guide to Understanding and Restoring Global Aquatic Biodiversity and Fishery Resources, Washington, DC: Island Press, 2007.

Nicolas Hulot, Phillippe Bourseiller, Steve Bloom, Gilles Martin, and Cal Vornberger
One Planet: A Celebration of Biodiversity, New York: Harry N. Abrams, 2006.

Malcolm Hunter and James P. Gibbs
Fundamentals of Conservation Biology, Malden, MA: Blackwell, 2006.

Christian Lévêque and Jean-Claude Mounolou Wiley — *Biodiversity*, New York: John Wiley & Sons, 2004.

Thomas E. Lovejoy and Lee Hannah, eds. — *Climate Change and Biodiversity*, New Haven, CT: Yale University Press, 2006.

Thomas O. McShane and Michael P. Wells, eds. — *Getting Biodiversity Projects to Work: Towards More Effective Conservation and Development*, New York: Columbia University Press, 2004.

Dorothy Hinshaw Patent and William Munoz — *Biodiversity*, Winnepeg, MB, Canada: Clarion Books, 2003.

Justina Ray, Kent Redford, Robert Steneck, and Joel Berger, eds. — *Large Carnivores and the Conservation of Biodiversity: Biodiversity*, Washington, DC: Island Press, 2005.

David Storch, Pablo Marquet, and James Brown, eds. — *Scaling Biodiversity*, Cambridge, U.K.: Cambridge University Press, 2007.

Crispin Tickell, Rupert F. G. Ormond, John D. Gage, and Martin V. Angel, eds. — *Marine Biodiversity: Patterns and Processes*, Cambridge, U.K.: Cambridge University Press, 2005.

John Vandermeer, Ivette Perfecto, and Vandana Shiva — *Breakfast of Biodiversity: The Political Ecology of Rain Forest Destruction*, Oakland, CA: Food First, 2005.

Periodicals

ABC News "Humans Spur Worst Extinctions Since Dinosaurs," March 21, 2006. www.abc.net.au/news/newsitems/ 200603/s1596740.htm.

Jennifer Barone "The Coldest Hotbed Ever: The Antarctic Seas Are Boiling Over with Biodiversity," *Discover*, August 2007, Vol. 28, Iss. 8, p. 12.

C. Brownlee "Life Underfoot: Microbial Biodiversity Takes Surprising Twist," *Science News*, January 14, 2006, Vol. 169, Iss. 2, p. 21.

The Economist (U.S.) "Fathoming Out Evolution; Biodiversity," May 19, 2007, Vol. 383, Iss. 8529, p. 83.

Robin Eisman "Plant a Garden for Biodiversity: As the World's Temperatures Change, Many Species of Birds, Bees and Butterflies Will Lose Their Feeding and Breeding Grounds. You Can Help These Pollinators and, in Turn the Ecological Cycle on Which We All Depend, by Planning Next Year's Garden as a Source of Food and Shelter for These Important Creatures," *Natural Life*, September–October 2006, p. 22.

Sigmar Gabriel "Biodiversity 'Fundamental' to Economics," *BBC News*, March 9, 2007. http://news.bbc.co.uk/2/hi/science/ nature/6432217.stm.

Geographical "Biodiversity: Almost All Large-Scale Human Activity Has an Impact on Nature," May 2007, Vol. 79, Iss. 5, p. 16.

Robert Gillespie and David Hill "Habitat Banking: A New Look at Nature and Development Mitigation," *Town and Country Planning*, April 2007, Vol. 76, Iss. 4, p. 121.

Anne Johnson "Cradle-to-Cradle Design," *Packaging Digest*, April 2007, Vol. 44, Iss. 4, p. 30.

Belden C. Lane "Biodiversity and The Holy Trinity: Each Species Was Created by the Same Hand of God that Made Us," *America*, December 17, 2001, Vol. 185, Iss. 20, p. 7.

Elizabeth Lindstrom "Edward O. Wilson: Turn Off the iPod . . . Tune in to Nature," *Odyssey*, April 2007, Vol. 16, Iss. 4, p. 34.

Reed Mangels "FAO Reports that Livestock Is a Major Contributor to Serious Environmental Problems Worldwide," *Vegetarian Journal*, April–June 2007, Vol. 26, Iss. 2, p. 20.

Andrew May and David Smart "Arable Farming and Biodiversity: Can the Two Coexist?" *Geography Review*, March 2006, Vol. 19, Iss. 4, p. 24.

Sean Nee "More than Meets the Eye . . . ," *Nature*, June 24, 2004, Vol. 429, Iss. 6994, p. 804.

Andrew Nielsen   "The Importance of Biodiversity in Livestock Production," *Countryside & Small Stock Journal*, July–August 2007, Vol. 91, Iss. 4, p. 57.

Kenneth Noble   "Our Hand in the Future: What Can Be Done to Avert Mass Extinction on a Scale Not Seen since the Age of the Dinosaurs," *For a Change*, April–May 2004, Vol. 17, Iss. 2, p. 7.

Elissa Parker   "Conserving Private Lands," *Environmental Forum*, March–April 2007, Vol. 24, Iss. 2, p. 55.

Space Daily   "Biologists Produce Global Map of Plant Biodiversity," March 26, 2007.

Paritosh Srivastava   "Hanging in the Balance: Conserving Biodiversity," *UN Chronicle*, September–November 2005, Vol. 42, Iss. 3, p. 53.

Nuria Tef and Stefanie Free   "Biodiversity Hotspots: Earth Focus Takes a Close Look at Three: Western Australia, the Atlantic Forest in Brazil and South-west China," *Earth Focus One Planet-One Community*, spring 2006, Vol. 29, p. 7.

Time

"The State of the Planet: The Good News: Population Growth Is Slowing, Life Expectancy Is Rising, and the Hole in the Ozone Layer, Which Shields Us from Ultraviolet Rays, Is Expected to Shrink. But Our Climate and Biodiversity Are in Peril, and Food and Water Supplies Will Be Tight," August 26, 2002, Vol. 160, Iss. 9, p. A15.

Hugh Warwick

"The Garden Up Above: Advocates of Green Roofs Have Long Pointed to Their Abilities to Reduce Energy Consumption and Flood Risk, But as Hugh Warwick Discovers, They Are Also Proving to Be Storehouses of Biodiversity," *Geographical*, July 2007, Vol. 79, Iss. 7, p. 38.

Howard Youth

"Winged Messengers: Does Habitat Loss Signal Biodiversity's Death Knell? Destruction of Ecological Living Spaces Is the Greatest Threat to the Survival and Preservation of the Globe's Wide Array of Animal and Plant Species," *USA Today* (Magazine), November 2003, Vol. 132, Iss. 2702, p. 52.

Index

A

Affluent lifestyles, 169–170
African elephants, 73, 140
Agriculture
    biodiversity and, 103–104,
      125–126
    See also Industrial agriculture
Agrochemicals, 107
Amazon basin, 71, 82
Amazon ecosystem, 155
Apiary Inspectors of America, 68
Aquaculture, 118

B

Bangladesh, 104–105
Bee diversity, 68
BIO 2003, 124
Biodiversity
    agriculture and, 103–104,
      125–126
    array of, 28
    biotechnology vs., 124–127
    cataloging, 51–52
    concentration of, 125
    conserving, 28
    cycles of, 63–66
    economic value of, 29–30
    ecosystems and, 17–18, 45–52,
      155–156
    fundamental components of,
      125
    high-yield industrial agricul-
      ture and, 121–123
    hotspots, 135–137
    importance, 21, 43, 114
    medicines and, 31–32
    national strategy, 148

    natural design principles and,
      160
    natural resources and, 21
    optimism about, 157–158
    organic farming and, 100–102,
      122–123
    overview, 21–22
    pollinators, 69
    population growth and, 167–
      169
    protecting, 18
    research on, 45–46
    scientific community and, 16
    sustainable use of, 148–153
    united effort, 38
    U.S. Agency for International
      Development (USAID),
      28–29
    in U.S. public parks, 133–134
    value of, 146, 155–157
Biodiversity and Conservation
    (Bryant), 18
Biodiversity loss, 16–17
    call for action, 24–25
    overstatement, 53
    rate, 25–27
    reasons, 71
    scientific study, 43–52
    threatened species, 27
    Wright/Muller-Lau study,
      53–62
Biodiversity Project, 179
Biodiversity prospecting, 22–23,
    141–142
Biodiversity Support Program, 179
Biological diversity, 16
Biotechnology
    biodiversity vs., 124–127

industrial agriculture and, 112–117

Biotropica (journal), 54, 58

Birds, 27, 91–93

Brazil, 82, 158

Bristol-Meyers-Squib, 22

Brown, Lester, 171

Bryant, Peter, 18

Bt corn pollen, 136–127

C

California, 171–172

CCD (Colony Collapse Disorder), 68

Center for Biodiversity Conservation, 180

Center for Global Food Issues, 12

Centre for Natural Products Research (Singapore), 22

CI (Conservation International), 22, 33, 36, 136–137, 177

CITES (Convention on International Trade in Endangered Species), 140, 142

Clayquot Sound, 150

Clean Air Act, 34

Clean Water Act, 34

Climate Change and Biodiversity (Lovejoy), 85

Climate scenarios, 97

Colony Collapse Disorder (CCD), 68

Commercial fishing, 128–130, 145, 166

Common Terns, 91–92

Community level partnerships, 37

Compendium of Fossil Marine Animal Genera (Sepkoski), 64

Conference of Parties (COP), 151

Conservation

ecosystem approach to, 148–149

In- vs. Ex-Situ, 148

species, 35–36

Conservation International (CI), 22, 33, 36, 136–137, 177

Consumables, 161

Convention on Biological Diversity, 18, 146–153

Convention on International Trade in Endangered Species (CITES), 140, 142

Convention on the Law of the Sea, 120

Cooperative Wholesale Association (Great Britain), 122

COP (Conference of Parties), 151

Coral reefs, 86, 88

Costa Rica, 73

Forestry Law (1996), 149

Merk, biodiversity prospecting in, 141–142

Crop

disasters, 114

diversity, 104–105

pollination, 69

production, 69

D

Defenders of Wildlife, 38

Deforestation, 82–83, 155–156

organic farming and, 122–123

rural growth rates, 54–55

Democratic Republic of Congo, 61

Developing countries, 176

financing, technical support for, 151–152

gender and, 176–178

Diversitas, 26

Durables, 161

E

Eastern Meadowlarks, 91
Ecological Society of America
(ESA), 180
Ecology, 159–160
Economic development, 138–139,
150–153
Ecosystem services, 52, 136–137
Ecosystems, 21
  Amazon, 155
  biodiversity and, 17–18, 45–
  52, 155–156
  complementarity model, 47
  idosyncratic model, 46–47
  importance, 44–45
  redundancy model, 46
  research on, 45–46
  species diversity, 43
Ecotourism, 140–141
Edible plants, 29
Endangered Species Act (ESA), 34
Environmental protection programs, 129
Environmentalist exaggerations,
126–127
ESA (Ecological Society of
America), 180
Evening Grosbeaks, 91
Extinction
  impact, 156–157
  mass, 26, 34, 167
  natural process, 17–18
  prevention, 98
  species, 16–17

F

Fish stocks, 39, 42, 75–79, 118–
120, 128–130, 145, 164
  See also Marine biodiversity
Food and Agriculture Organization (FAO), 119, 180–181

Ford, Harrison, 33, 36
Forests, 30
  old vs. secondary growth,
  58–60
  Wright/Muller-Lau study,
  58–60
  See also Rainforests; Tropical
  forests
Fossil diversity cycle, 64–66
Future Harvest, 158
The Future of Life (Wilson), 36
*The Future of Tropical Forest Spe-
cies* (Wright, Muller-Landau), 54

G

The Gaia Hypothesis (Lovelock),
123
GEF (Global Environment
Facility), 152
Gender, in developing countries,
176–178
Genetic homogenization, modern
agriculture, 105–105
Genetically modified (GM) crops,
113–117
  consequences, 115–116
  purpose, 117
  solutions, 116
Glaxo Wellcome, 22
Global Climate Change convention, 139–140
Global climate change study,
95–96
Global Environment Facility
(GEF), 152
Global warming, 95, 139–140
  causes, 17, 111
  combating, 30
  effects, 71, 86, 90–93
  marine life and, 27
  time lag, 57

Gordon and Betty Moore Foundation, 36

Greater Scaup, 91

Green development, 138–144
  evaluating, 142–144
  uncertain future, 144

Green Revolution, 104, 121

Greenpeace, 121, 124

H

H. John Heinz III Center for Science, Economics and the Environment, 85

Habitat degradation, 35

Honoring the sacred, 162–163

I

ICUN (International Union for the Conservation of Nature and Natural Resources), 16, 176, 181

Illegal markets, 72

India, 143

Indonesia, 143–144

Industrial agriculture, 103–111
  agrochemicals, 107
  biodiversity, 103–104
  biotechnology, 112–117
  chemical fertilizers, 110–111
  crop replacement, 108
  environmental problems, 109–112
  farm component assemblage, 107
  fertilizer nutrients, 111
  monoculture, 105–108
  nutrient cycles, 107
  pesticides, 106, 110
  pests, 107–109
  yield loss, 109

Insects, invertebrates, 27–28

Intergovernmental Panel on Climate Change (IPCC), 26, 97

International efforts, 22

International Food Policy Research Institute, 122, 176

International Plan of Action to Prevent, Deter and Eliminate Unreported and Unregulated Fishing, 119–120

International Union for the Conservation of Nature and Natural Resources (ICUN), 16, 176, 181

IPCC (Intergovernmental Panel on Climate Change), 26, 97

K

Kenya, 140–141, 174

Kenya Wildlife Service (KWS), 142

Keystone species, 46–47

Kiunga National Marine Reserve, 174

Kyoto Protocol, 172

L

Lady's slipper orchid, 73

Lake Manyara Biosphere Reserve, 150

Lake Tanganyika Catchment Reforestation and Education (TACARE), 177

Land mammals, threatened, 27

Landowner incentives, 37

Little Blue Herons, 92

Logging, 17, 27, 58, 71–72, 91–92, 133

Lovejoy, Thomas, 85

Lovelock, James, 123

M

Magnuson-Stevens Fishery Conservation and Management Act, 165

Mangroves, 83–84

Marine biodiversity, 78–79
  commercial fishing, 128–130, 145
  data, 39–41
  ecosystems vs. species preservation, 41–42
  government policy, 41–42
  importance, 38–39
  Jamaica study, 40
  overfishing problem, 118–120
  protections, 165–166
  status, 164–165
  threatened, 27

Marine Life Protection Act (1999), 165

Marine Protected Areas (MPAs), 118–119

Mass extinction, 26, 34, 168

Mauritius, 71–72

Mauritius kestrel, 73

McKee, Jeffrey, 167–170, 172–173

Medicines, plants and, 22, 29, 31–32

Merk, 141–143

Mexico, 149, 150–151, 177

Monoculture agriculture, 105–108

Monsanto, 113

Monteverde Cloud Forest Reserve, 96

MPAs (Marine Protected Areas), 118–119

Muller, Richard, 63–66

Muller-Landau, Helene, 53–62

N

NABIN (North American Biodiversity Information Network), 182

National Audubon Society (NAS), 89, 181

National biodiversity strategy, 148

National Center for Atmospheric Research, 86

National Center of Ecological Analysis and Synthesis (NCEAS), 75–76

National Council for Science and the Environment (NCSE), 181

National Institutes of Health, 22

National Oceanic and Atmospheric Administration, 86

National Park Service, 37

National Research Council, 127

National Resource Defense Council (NRDC), 165–166

National Science Foundation, 75

National Wildlife Federation, 172

Natural design principles, 159–163
  biodiversity and, 160
  consumables, durables, unmarketables, 161–162
  defining characteristics, 160
  honoring the sacred, 162–163

Natural resources, 21

The Nature Conservancy (TNC), 37, 76, 182–183

Nature (journal), 22, 63–64, 95–96, 170

NCSE (National Council for Science and the Environment), 181

NECEAS (National Center of Ecological Analysis and Synthesis), 75–76

North American Biodiversity Information Network (NABIN), 182

Northern Bobwhite, 90

Northern Pintail, 91

NRDC (National Resource Defense Council), 165–166

O

Ocean acidification, 85–89
Organic farming, 100–102, 122–123

P

Percy Schmeise case, 113
Pesticides, 106, 110
Plants
    diversity, 114
    edible, 29
    medicines from, 22, 29, 31–32
    threatened, 27
Population Action International, 175
Population, human, 17, 33
    growth, 167–169, 172–173, 175
    resources for, 145–146
    settlement patterns, 146
    world, 175
Prescription drugs, 22
Private lands, 133
Private sector, 36–38
Project Tiger, India, 142

R

Rainforests, 81–82, 155–158
Red List, World Conservation Union, 35
Regional Sea Conventions, 120
Reptiles, amphibians, 27
Research Institute for Organic Agriculture, 101
Rhode, Robert, 63–66
Rice ecosystems, 150
The Riddled Chain: Chance, Coincidence, and Chaos in Human Evolution (McKee), 168–169
Rio Summit, 152

Roosevelt, Theodore, 132
Royal Botanical Gardens, 73
Rufous Hummingbird, 92
Rural growth rates, deforestation and, 54–55

S

Science and technology, 38
Science (journal), 75, 101, 128
Seed Savers Exchange, 183
Sepkoski, Jack, 64
Sian Ka'an Biosphere Reserve, 150–151
Sierra Club, 172
Smithsonian Tropical Research Institute, 53–54
Snow Buntings, 92
Soil fertility, 100
Soufrière Marine Management Area, 149
Sparing Nature (McKee), 167–169, 173
Species
    conservation of, 35–36
    diversity of, 43
    ecosystems, 43
    extinction of, 16–17
    functional groups, 45
    keystone, 46–47
    threatened, endangered, 27–28, 34, 91–93
Suriname, 22
Sustainable development, 73–74, 148–153

T

TACRE (Lake Tanganyika Catchment Reforestation and Education), 177
Tanzania, 150

TNC (The Nature Conservancy), 37, 76, 182–183

Transgenic crops, 113

Tropical forests, 32, 53–54
  deforestation threats, 82–83
  evolution of, 80–81
  mangroves, 83–84

Tropical rice ecosystems, 150

20 Common Birds in Decline (Audubon), 91–93

U

Uganda, 149

UN Convention on Biological Diversity, 43

UN Population Fund, 172

UNEP Global Programme of Action for the Protection of the Marine Environment from Land based Activities, 120

United Nations Development Programme (UNDP), 151

United Nations Environment Programme (UNEP), 36, 118–120, 152, 183

United Nations World Food Program, 116

United States, threatened and endangered species, 27, 34

Unmarketables, 162

U.S. Agency for International Development (USAID), biodiversity efforts, 28–29

U.S. Department of Agriculture, 33, 69

U.S. Department of the Interior, 36

USA Today (newspaper), 128–129

V

The Value of Medicines (PhRMA report), 33

W

Whip-poor-wills, 92

Who Will Feed China? (Brown), 171

Wild bird populations
  habitat losses, 92–93
  long-term outlook, 93–94
  threatened species, 91–92

Wild seafood, 74

Wilderness Act of 1964, 132

Wilderness preservation, 132–134

Wilson, Edward, 36

Women, 176–178

World Bank, 152

World Conservation Monitoring Centre, 119, 183

World Conservation Trust, 122

World Conservation Union, 35, 158

World Summit on Sustainable Development (2002), 118

World Wildlife Fund, 174

Wright, Joseph, 53–62

Wright/Muller-Landau study, 53–62
  caveats, 55–57
  conclusions, 54–55
  continued research, 61
  critics, 55–61
  data vacuum, 59
  old vs. secondary growth forest, 58–60

Y

Yellowstone National Park, 37, 132